Musings
Verses Across the Year 2008

by
Elizabeth Clayton

Order this book online at www.trafford.com
or email orders@trafford.com

Most Trafford titles are also available at major online book retailers.

Cover Design/Artwork: Elizabeth Clayton and Lynn O. Waltman
Designed by: Elizabeth Clayton
Photography: Lynn O. Waltman
Editor: Lynn O. Waltman

Print information available on the last page.

ISBN: 978-1-4269-2026-4 (sc)

Trafford rev. 03/27/2021

 www.trafford.com

North America & international
toll-free: 844-688-6899 (USA & Canada)
fax: 812 355 4082

The title for the work, <u>Musings</u>, is in part, "across the year 2008", referenced to a poignant expression, repeatedly offered each Christmas, from one of my mother's dearest friends: the lady who helped her forty-two years and more, in all domestic needs. She would say, at the exchanging of gifts "… and I thank you for all you have done for me 'across this year'."

Table of Contents

This book is dedicated, lovingly,
to my mother,
Mae Belle Buckles Derrick,
my gentle firelighter, whom I never
heard laugh, but gave me
the color of rose.

August 4, 2009

Foreword

Elizabeth Clayton's *Musings*, her poetry collection from 2008, takes the reader through the seasons from winter to spring, from spring through summer, and finally through Autumn to Christmastide. She ends, as Tennyson did *In Memoriam* with that holiday season which offers hope and rebirth in the middle of the darkest, coldest night. That is a fitting ending (and new beginning) for her and for her readers. Living with her bipolar condition means at times that the nights are dark and long, but even in the winter snows, she manages to find buttercup blossoms, roses woven into the carpet, light from unexpected sources.

And these unexpected moments of grace enlighten the poetry. These images are among her strengths as a poet. She finds in the simplest of objects, the quotidian repetition of hours and activities, the visits with friends, and in her memories, the joy that sustains. As she says in one poem:

> We hold no moment, but imbibe freely,
> In the masterful half-smile
> Of the reality of tense.

Along with the images, her free verse form allows the ideas and images to work together to make shape. Her poems have an internal rhythm and structure which often complements the thought thoroughly. The words take shape, and the shape enhances the words. At times playful, at times prayerful, at time reflective and at time reactive, the poems work to capture the ephemeral with similes and syntax. Beyond that, the poet in her poems leads us to the realization that she, and in turn, each of us, embodies those ideas within the living structure of our lives and bodies. We are, she reminds us, living symbols. Late in the collection, she writes:

> When the sunlight fails to fall lightly,
> Faintly, on the cool October leaves
> In these, its final hours,
> I will draw the door and the season of cold
> Will be with us—
> We each, as in all seasons, microcosms
> Of this experience we call
> Being, existence, in which we
> Live and in which
> We die...

"Being," living, dying—all three states are present throughout the year's meditations. Rounding out many of the poems is the poet's attention to "the little death," sleep, which is such a precious commodity and powerful image in her condition. Often in the notations at the end of the verse, the provenance of the poem we have just read, she tells us that the words come from "the deepest night," "at faintest daybreak," or after a "night's conversation." But these poems are not dark, not ever completely, because verses also arise, we are told in at least one instance, at "about eight o'clock am, Beauty of sunshine in the outside cold." And even the darkest night, can end with promise: "I looked to the balcony and light was/Faintly promising—/Somehow, Friend, I had passed the night. . ." So all of life's facets reflect truth—the dark and the light.

And the readers are invited to be her friends as they read through the hours, the days, the months, the seasons of this collection. These are "musings" as the title suggests, thoughts. But the word also echoes the deeper image of the Muses, those mythological women of inspiration who implanted thoughts in human minds and gave rise to the creative arts. Elizabeth Clayton at once receives these seedling thoughts and lets them grow, and also transmits these "musings" to the readers, perhaps to nurture their own new creative growth.

David G. Miller
May 2009

Acknowledgements

Acknowledgement remarks to this volume of poetry are truly modest, for there is most to be best said in Emily Dickinson's borrowed remark from one of her verses: "... my letter to the world that never wrote to me." My verses in "Musings..." is a song from one of my years, out myself, with few readers, those with criticisms or helpful suggestions. While I enjoy a great number and variety of friends, they are generous to occasionally ask about my poetry, but do not, will not read it. And since I am not a "group" person or "cluber," I have few companionable colleagues.

And so left is faithful Ora Steele, careful in all things— clerical and finishings, but a special appreciation is given to my physician and friend, Dr. John Norton of The University of Mississippi Medical Center, Jackson, Mississippi, who catches at every opportunity to encourage pulling myself out of my closeted spirit—to free, and in revealing, know acknowledgement and satisfaction. Without his encouragement and constancy in suggestion and direction, my writings would have come to be no more than anecdotal reflections.

I must also express a special gratitude to Dr. David Miller, my friend and chair to the Department of English at the small liberal arts university, Mississippi College, in Clinton, Mississippi, where he invited me to join his faculty as an adjunct instructor. The entire experience was delightful, and he very carefully read and thoughtfully evaluated "Musings…" for me, preparing the foreword; I am indebted to him for this gesture of friendship.

And finally, there are some few readers who keep apprised of my work, to often send good wishes and helpful instructions, especially my nephew, Jason: great wealth is his with such kin and friends—and roses to my dear friend Lynn Waltman for preparations for publication.

Out of myself, to the world, I have sung with little instruction, beams, arches or buttressing, within the music I most enjoy—silence: a song of thoughtful sentiment which is a partial record of soul in the tryst of will and circumstance.

Elizabeth
June 18, 2009

Preface

Prefacing thought, especially when there are those personally intimate and often with strong emotional underpaintings, can gather into a requiring task, to say "everything that should be said, and not anything that should not be said." My collection of all verses written in 2008, "my musings," suggests most of my usual stances, but particularly, the cycling of my moods, and the subject areas particular to them, always including the matter of impermanence.

Bipolar intensity renders each piece a climatic statement, an image within a mood, as if it be the "last word." I have added notes, when appropriate, to help balance the sentiment so that reviewing these pieces will not leave the reader fatigued or press him into a complexion that would be an unsatisfied one.

Free verse is my choice of vehicle for expression, for in quiet rebellion, I do not wish even conventional restrictions. My greatest concern is the pensiveness, the negativism, the dark presence, overmuch of the verses, that they are disproportionately so, even with the manic outbursts describing my absolute joy in the feast of life, when I can catch it; and there are periods of moderation when experiencing life falls more within the "norm"—but still, the dark is most present.

Routine events and thought that occur within their seasons, alongside lifelong philosophical "joustings" concerning problematic areas in being are the subjects I pen—as they are perceived by me in the strange milieu of my psyche. To some, this circumstance may seem too narcissistic, too much "meism" in a world of problems and situations of much more importance—and which have greater merit and worth, immediacy and spirited movement—all much "more" than the very private world through which I position my steps;—but, then, I offer only my own experience with the hope that (to rephrase Faulkner), I may leave something in the heart that was not there before.

When I do enter into gentle reverie or perceive a sound, a color, a fragrance or form which ignites a chain of thought, leading very often to a verse, the time is always summer—warm, bright, colorful, long and unstructured, and unending—that which could be seen in such a present. But the beginning of a year, to be recorded throughout in verse, through sentiments' script or no, begins in winter; and so I am thoughtful to include several earlier winter verses, for they lie deep within me, my memory chamber, my grandly appointed cathedral of feeling—rich of years and the condiments to life they provide. They were experienced in very negative arrangements, those which, together became impetus to the ensuring saga of our family through a journey quite extraordinaire—and responsible for much of the reservoir of feeling I now hold.

The winters were, in a word, cruel, and gave us all cause to take joy in beauty, wherever it could be found: in berries and melons, flowers and rainfall, the towering pine, the enduring cedar—and ultimately, to mourn their passing, as that inside ourselves, an occurring which was must to be, for we, innocent wayfarers, left large portions of our own beauty, quite unreviewed or recognized, to metamorphose into further, different—distance modes of feeling and expression. These verses are, verily, jewel-like to me, my treasures, of time past without which "Musings ... 2008" would not have taken form. Their poignant sentiments, their bittersweet hues, their now failing light leave me open to the full of each day, those in 2008 now passed over, and ever towardward.

As brilliant sunlight through a crystal piece, I hope excerpts from my thoughts appear more beautiful, almost fanciful, to have been worded, fashioned again, having passed through my particular hours of nourishing pathos and reflections upon it.

Elizabeth
January 24, 2009

Giving Jewels:
Wetted Ebony Into Lighted
Grey
The womb is dark and unknowing, the world lighted but
filled with shadows,
clouds, and the misty veil of winds and rain—and voices
often not in pleasing understandings.

Excerpt from _I, Elizabeth_
(Vignette Four)

The seasons, in the rural, had each, its unique beauty, its special call to me. There were happy snatches from the grief—animals, woodfires, heavy quilts, hand stitched, Christmas, church, Vacation Bible School, revivals; there was preparation for church, an almost frenzy of activity to look and be our best, and in the evenings, at home, family alter. The ebbing and flowing included small disasters, of course, and they touched me also: the unwanted pregnancy and accepted birth of my youngest brother, the ice storm in 1951 which required my father to continuously scavenge for wood to keep a one fireplace affording heat; I remember his eyes, for he became snowblind from the excessive glare of the light of day on snow all over, everywhere, for days. In all his chores, however, I remember his tender lessons, showing us how to catch and roast birds, a kind of happy, engaging activity pulled forth from the intolerable circumstance.

Inside Images

Images crowd, bringing the first car,
The old, cold school,
Afternoons in winter,
As a choir of women dying,
Their tears and sighs in my hearing now,
Their mortality usurped by sentiment that
Wills to speak,
And I hear, replies out of quick travail,
Into my ready voice,
Pressing my lips to passion, willing and
Impatient;
But the divide of awareness closets the
Rounding of my sound,
And I smile and speak with full timbre
To the vendors,
Only to know sighs, after tears,
Of indescribable beauty,
My longing ought but reachings
In silent gestures, becoming a gentle berceuse
Dressing my waiting certain—patient closure.

Elizabeth, waiting tires at Firestone, Northside, Jackson,
Mississippi—
I knew that I was near to full hallucination,
Or merely responding (intense), naturally
For me to a significant stimulus—
July 2, 2001

4

Impotent Baskets

So much we cannot know,
and so we do not know.
Stars cannot gather into baskets,
however open and receiving,
for thought and study,
to explain their roundness,
or their points' arranging,
but we to only,
with understanding of their light appearing,
know their constancy and giving.

-Written to comfort Elva Giddings,
a condolence following her son's unfortunate death, 2000

Into Oxford, One

There is captured in the grief of a soul,
beauty,
as in fire,
leaping,
even into its passing,
this captured beauty,
incomparable.

Into Oxford, Two

And there rose to my gaze
the cold knot of birds;
and just at my attention,
they shattered,
into the knot's funeral pattern,
spreading of darkened gold dust,
as having been touched suddenly
by an eager, spirited breath
that wandered on,
an innocent, natural Pippa.

Winter

Winter came to me today.
I saw blackbirds fly, and I felt the self
that walks behind the promenade
of white puffs of chilled breath,
whistling, along a silent, still path
to warm hearth-hours.

Brought Back

Leaving the wealth of late summer dreams,
I can smell and taste again
cold, set coffee:
together there were baked sweet potato peels,
with their blackened sugar,
among the day's cinders.
There was neither flower not lamp,
but only that which the cold daylight allowed.
The poverty of the setting energized us,
and we waited,
with innocent press, for the years to unfold,
and to bring us, again,
to remembrance.

September Dreams

I have dreamed,
and I have forgotten,
but to find September again,
a time of gold and burgundy
in bunching chrysanthemum faces,
of riding a sleigh of autumn winds;
of hearing earliest hearth hours
calling out of smoke
journeying upward
from today's burning leaves.
Forgotten dreams,
in their clever accessibility,
are found again,
their sealed door
unlocked by September's haunting face
and her enchanting repertoire
of voiced silence,
her sentiment too great
to serve a generous moment,
but rather to rise with the sun,
and to lie down with his pardoned glory
-with these dreams,
to open the fragrance of darkness,
and breathe unto rapture night sweet olive,
to glimpse,
and reach to touch,
the summer evening moth
that flies into its flame of certain dark.

Winter Peace

The clock continues past coffee in its cup
-morningtime in December,
and the sun appears almost as an afterthought;
in a suede exchange, deep red,
generous poinsettia compensates,
in her feathered leaf robe,
flowing, beautiful.
And silence falls about
like the segmented journey of reluctant leaves.
Distant traffic haloes the quiet,
while thoughts smile out on a carpet of brown,
knowing that within the long sleep
lies the white evergreen of winter peace.

Arabesque

Light opened onto morning
with a clarion stillness,
shadows quiet
so that I knew the pleasure of gentle death;
for a long moment
the fixed orchestration held,
as surprise and awe,
hurt and disbelief.
Harmony swelled,
to find new expression in soft movement,
leaves drawing autumn pictures,
gold fantasias of lost seasons,
making memory that waits
with the finishing warmth
in the arabesque of fallen summer.

Winter Day

Winter day,
cold breath,
in and out,
cold chimes ringing;
grey gargoyle shadows guarding,
on every corner,
the fragile, hesitating sunlight
that unveils stick trees,
India ink spilled against its pallored being:
the cold hour is sounded,
a trumpet's song of ten,
a chronicle of cold hours
that advance out of yesterday,
painting scenes,
sewing velvet around the edges,
the thread of hope securing gold tassels
which hang like shining teardrops,
finishing the piece;
we are dead in the cold,
our spirits wrestling with heavy moments
of conclusion and decay,
that, with the ember of yesterday,
may pulsate into the grace of new fire.
Winter day,
cold winds, arranging umbers,
gathering humble blue into grey,
holding under,
within,
the fire of eternity's deep well,
our patient struggle drawing a rose
whose yearning
will open her petals into new summer.

A Road

In full,
rich darkness,
a nightingale came to me,
its wings tipped in autumn gold,
and about its neck
wore a silk flame, flowing.
In the season's cool,
it sang,
with periwinkle freshness
and a fullness of twilight,
as stars visiting each other,
into the wideness of midnight.
The beauty of the fancy fell upon me,
and I felt,
of my care,
comforted.
The night grew,
with the bird weaving into its face,
finally into the greater,
faithful dark,
its song becoming a road out of self,
and silent warring.

Play

The soil and a stick;
playfulness and laughter,
and voila,
there is a circle and a game.
The marble is in our hands
and we can move it;
and if we do not score
we are advised of the shooter,
and so stand strong in our certitude.
But that is not always the way;
yet we continue to shoot,
leaning forward as we touch and move.

Chilled Crocks

Woodfire and smoke,
berries smiling brightly
through rain of constant falling,
cold and cold,
continuous reaching damp,
our southern face ruddy and grim,
beyond sunlight's cheer,
with smallest comforts.
Greatest joy pours out
from chilled crocks of fabled summer.

Early childhood memory of the cruel winters—
Tasting the mustiness of decay in ripe,
late summer fruit
found the promise of autumn's wild plum.
And, in place is a quieted sun
that allows nights which touch dust cool
and leaves to wear dull green jackets.
Harmony hurries the seasons in and out,
and yet surprise hangs on newly painted leaves,
and frost and cold and greeted,
in all innocence, as curious.
And so,
our hearts are romanced by the calendar,
and we consent to embraces
of color and fragrance and touch,
being altogether cuckolded
by the draught of forgetfulness.

Autumn Notes: One

Late afternoon, November 11, 1999
Mamma and Daddy

The afternoon sun has found my trees,
and I sit in these rooms, alone,
to watch it die.
The glow is still, waiting the silence,
and I hear amber voices that speak
with soft assurances,
and remind that the harvest moon
can be my gold.

Autumn Notes: Two

Late afternoon, November 11, 1999
With Me, Wayne, Marion and David

Echoes sound of autumns past, of small,
clustered blue-black grapes,
and the cold of the far pasture.
Smoke from pine and the delicious mystery
of night touched us eager voyagers;
fields lay in moonlight, exhausted and quiet
while food reigned with honor true.
Cold made of us able soldiers,
and we did battle with fervor,
securing the self, each, himself.
Across impatient years, echoes have found
our autumn selves, and we cannot
know of greater truth than
in echoes gold to the golden ear.

A Way

The sun glanced the furniture,
touching,
retreating,
and in its silent, lighted movement,
I heard memories that illuminated my being.
The memories spoke of life,
of light and shadow,
of the strong and the weak,
of the true good.
These visiting,
of silent, speaking lights,
allow to me a way.

Winter of January

Weary and sighing into what might be,
perhaps, a new moon's language,
we are passed through the winter of January,
it in the night, almost in secret,
putting away the quiet of festivals,
with polished silver and silk berries,
when windows could offer,
as the determined steps of obligatory walks,
only lifeless browns and greys,
days of wet and damp,
past hope, or beauty,
yet only ochered joy;
but we do hear, now,
songs form morning birds,
whose melodies have been saved away,
to be lost
through golden frost and December true;
but we do hear, their sounds falling
as the diamond rain of eager forsythia,
its fragile bells of yellow sparkling,
about its generous twines.
And thought presses toward fabled green,
sunlight, with more voice,
of Iberian ambered warm,
filling days with a beautiful strange familiarity;
umbers and shadows ride the hour's brow,
with patient haste, into forgetfulness,
and hands, which, in a lonely constancy,
wait, reaching fickle wares
into their draught of silence,
which of the whole, does not give back.

The guitar, the cold stall,
Molasses candy—
I cannot bear—

Song Cycle

Summer evening songs are familiar,
tonight,
sounding as childhood prayers,
softly,
as the touch of darkness.
Growth courts fulfillment,
to purpose harvest
that will fill ready baskets and barns,
to, with grape and grain,
pass beyond the bath of dark and light,
finding their gold and roundness
out of the womb of night,
following
after the travail, and debutance of day.

-a nice conceit,
the extended metaphor of recognition of
coming winter in the moments before sleep.

The MUSINGS

Winter

The hour had accomplished to exactly
Eleven thirty, and I stood in the
Almost dark, shadowed sitting room,
Under the voice of
Bocelli; the air was quiet and I received the
Full richness of his voice.
The moon, though outside his voice,
Poured equal wealth onto me as it
Painted in the majestic trees in its passing.
The objects on the patio,
Now below as I had moved upstairs,
Gradually danced into a familiar minuet,
With partial color and form.
My gown touched my body, my feet peeking
Out below, and I, fragranced of Provence's
Honey soap, enchanted the night.
How beautiful to be alive, aware, and yet, alone,
With my thought, for it held a castle,
Surely, of images, dreams, and wishes
Which could never come forward
In the sun's demanding true.
Ah, "little death"—you have a moment
When I do not wish your banishment to light and
Requiring—and all of its splendid trappings—
Stay while the music is not yet suggestive
Of conclusion, and all the mirrors smile
Their gentle; and I am a matron queen
Who does not pity the late wine
Of yesterday's fuchsia petunia,
But waltzes with the images, lifts to the dreams,
And bows in fealty to the wishes of her dark castle—

A moment, insane, but necessary nourishment
For, perhaps, my heart, alone, to greet the
Reality that will hear ring in the morrow's
Six o'clock —
Elizabeth
Undated, 2008

And I will sleep again,
In the new day,
As morning songbirds
Sing among cool dews;
And
As the sun in a slow constancy,
With the very integrity
Of the heart,
Begins its rising,
To grace all with
Its ever warmth,
Out of the East
Into its westward
Part—
Among these beauty
I
Will, again, sleep.

Elizabeth, undated

The smoke of temple incense,
Embroidering the ringing of small bells—
Neither these nor the rounding and
Painting of the pomegranate offers more peace than such moments
Of awareness
And thanksgiving, which flow out
My plume, to be
Humble, gently laid aside with a mood.

Elizabeth, part-song, undated

Comfort, on all sides, is truly
The dragon
In a moment,
Leaving us weary, or, at least as the mundane;
Without our passion, the lifting of a
Flower is difficult,
As hearing the joy in birdcalls,
Or the true peace in soft rainfall.
The butterfly becomes a jewel
Whose
Light eludes us,
The day, full content, its own death;
And a whistle, a stick, wet bamboo—an aria—
These can ignite to let free away
Our spirit, on wings
Of good passion carried in intention.
I smile on the duality, the paradox in full
Simplicity
Of the
Juxtaposition
Inside the gift of a day,
In its all wealth and poverties.

Elizabeth, an attachment, undated

I try to stay the past away from thought,
Away from feeling caught close
Inside my heart,
For this treasure of hurt
Is wounding
In its beauty and shadows to
All the bright of
New morning.

This collection of wisdoms,
Of
Shattering truth,
Illumines with a great
Dark
Which tears lessen and soften
But cannot complete
A purge that leaves
No stain.

Prayer

Elizabeth, undated

Buttercups

Hey Lord,
Thanks for the buttercups,
Turned up faces,
Their petals moving in the appearing soft,
Pink wind, like dolls in tender hands.
Thanks,
For they suggested to look, to see, and
Receive the loveliness of early
Summer sunflowers, and
Purple verbena;
I had not known where I wanted to be,
Only away from memory of the
Hurting exchange,
In which I felt weak and transparent,
And the multitude
Of my sins poured out crimson.
Hey Lord,
You knew before the deep, purple hurt,
And you let me know it,
But there was provided a pasture,
In sunlight, where colors touched me,
And peace fell like an ivory oil,
Into the purple hurt,
Diluting the pain,
Leaving me where I was content to be.

Elizabeth, undated
An early piece, brought out in 2008

When angels open doors or fling out window
Casements, they emit light from their presence,
To become, in time, apparitions that wander
To prophesy, to speak truths, to narrate,
To remind, and pronounce.
These beings are seen as images by few,
Ought poets, singers, the tortured mad,
But come to enter us all, presently, as
Consciousness, either covered, partially
Clothed, or fully aware, therefore adding
The great dissonance to all creation:
We become gods and men, having been
Anointed by those who serve holiness,
All truth, which cannot be, in mortal
Semantics, processed—gods and men
Alive to die.
Andso, I, midst multitudes of lamentations,
Yet the anguish of crucifixion, a jealous
God, for mortality is but an echo of the
Devine, spirit, our first in memory and
Pain in farewelling.

I, then, a jealous god, but not of material
Meats: nor do I wish the wealth, whatever
Its complexion, of any other, to be mine.
All that I wish is the bliss of repose, awake,
Time not holding the cup that runs over,
Of experience.
I am careful of the twilight, for it takes into the
Shadows the spirit of life: light.
And I am jealous of the larger seasons—the green,
The blush, the gold, the white—for they

Mirror our measured steps.
Jealousy spars with impermanence, and I
In full, whole spirit, am a god who wishes,
As does all consciousness, immortality.

Elizabeth, 2008

Give back to me—my hours, beautiful moments
Of generous good, contentment that is passing
In its laughter;
Give back the jewels of years and completion,
Of vigor and dreams and adventure—
For I am of the time ledgered to me.

If I could hold the moment in its fragile
Loveliness, know the wisdom of old, dead men,
With their hounds faithful in their service;
If I could follow the softer winds to bring them
Back with their freshness and promise of
Their morning hours,
I would be, indeed, a god, jealous always,
But placid in my negative that time would
Declare a rest, an island, and I would
Visit again and again, and not in reverie alone,
The gardens of the newborn aware.

These good would return in the image of
Appropriate angels bearing gifts flown
On the wind, whispers in the night,
As when the circle opened.

Elizabeth, January 5, 2008
A fancy

35

Winter, 2008

The time is January, and the hour just before daybreak;
In my heart, yet, it is spring, approaching
Morning bright,
For I have close, love.
Fairies make flowers larger, small animals
As very beastly kinds—
All because they are of qualities beautiful,
Close to good, close to love.
I then, am faery in early morning bright,
Having cast aside my morning veil
For a purpose I do not, cannot
Comprehend;
Love spins webs of beautiful colors,
Echoes and whispers of light,
A presence of larger good, with hope,
Pippa innocence and the returning,
Dying twilight.

Elizabeth
January 11, 2008, about 9:00 am
Feeling well since rising at 3:30 am

I will sketch an angel today, correct a French
Phrase, design my tapestry into a purse,
Take a flower to Nadine, and check on Judy,
Linda and Melba—

The rug has roses woven into it, of a
Pleasing pink hue—amazing to find it
So late—

37

Thoughts, thoughts, and thoughts,
Tumbling over and about my pen;
How does one truly record
The musings of the full heart—
In words, but more in symbolic
Gestures
Known only to he who
Muses and he who knows of the
Very existing spirit between.
Elizabeth, January 11, 2008
7:45 am

We need, then, not to, with clever finesse, cover our eyes.

Light is dallying with the hour,
And verities spar with my
Consciousness;
To be awake is to know truth
In darkness,
Heartful truth.
But light in its splendor
Illumines the fire of the truth in dark,
In brightest, glowing day.

Elizabeth, January 11, 2008
About 7:30 am

Piercing light, though small,
Through my south trees—

38

Angel Presence

I bathed in early morning
With Michelle's gift
Of
Christmas soap,
Leaving her sentiment attached:
So sweet the hearted
Fragrance of caring
Earthly angels.

Elizabeth, January 11, 2008
About 6:30 am

With Thought

I am whining away my days,
Begging off life;
Thoughtful love hangs at a distance,
And I have nothing in my hand except
Whispers of fancy and the embellished
Yesterday.
I press to will,
And the music's sounds wound,
Having struck, like a strong
Wind against my back;
But I found its beauty, and the troth
Was honored again,
Will into pain and beauty,
Curious paradox that only the seasons can rival:
Beauty wedded, ever, to loss.

The sweetest sword, to strike into one's deep,
Only enough that it come again.

Elizabeth, January 14, 2008, 6:15 am
Under Bocelli's voice, after
Wellness enough to appraise my thought
And mood—long time down
This time; Dr. Norton at 12:45 today—

All that I know, and all that I feel
Lies out before me in flowing fashion;
The meadow in first morning, the cloth with
Appointments of wheat and grape,
The napkin with communion stains, yet, bright
Blood drops.
These images warm and clothe me,
Dress me queenly as I, the humble Ester;
Whispering verses of joy in beauty,
Strength in substance, purity of spirit,
Just given over.
Days and days, thoughts and thoughts
Move our hours, and we are
Lost in the noble, the honorable,
And caught in the trivial—
Working in us, our hearts' chambers,
Full of purpose and composure,
No matter their sources,
For such is to be of good, doctrine and writ,
Tenet and oblations, lifted—all aside—
For it is of good that we be, and that we see,
To feel and know, fullest blessing.

A prayer in noontime, addressing our philosophical
Matters that really do not concern as the heart
Is subject to reaching toward the good,
No matter the path.

Elizabeth, January 17, 2008

Spiders Weave (Morning Notes, One)

Spiders weave in absence and moonlight,
In emptinesses, in openings
Without centers,
Not to soon be closed.
In autumn days, in September and mourning,
Webs come to geister in falling sunlight;
When noon has announced, when
Summer warmth finds its medes,
When radiance is already a longing,
Spiders weave.

And when words are woven, they, with careless indignities,
At moments unpromised, when offending
Seems the better part,
They show shadows to fall,
And stars become deep wells, weeping unto, dark
Tears; swirlings of grey look up to accept
Birds wide, covering, great fans bringing
Silences, frozen and a winter's dead,
Absent of hue, these flying with branches which
Do not bud or leaf.

Elizabeth, July 2, 2001
Waiting for tires at
Firestone, on Northside—

42

Remembering the weaving image, the spider, but at the tire
Store, yet another image out of relationships—

Sunday morning, July 1, 2001, beauty in overcast moments,
Reminding, always, my darkly pensive heart, moments passing,
Reaching into a now that, somehow, always has been, a time
Of their farewells and remembering.

I believe this piece is the "lost" "Morning Notes, One" of the three
Part series—
Elizabeth, transcribed, January 24, 2008

Muse, Muse, sister spirit, comrade
Whose amour I share,
Come, come back to me;
Sit like softest little babies
On my lap, that I may love and touch your being,
Drawing strength from your innocence,
Yet the scarlet cord of reality.
For infant words are filled with wisdom,
Therefore truest beauty,
And I need, I wish in my emptiness
To be filled with the gold of first thought,
Ancient wanderings,
The now sayings of my life that all be gathered together in my
pen,
Words scripted, little babies of beautytruth,
Full issue out the impotently raging,
Yet yearning, biding
Of mine, my heart.

I feign an unableness, but it is an
Unhappy covering; I could be vapid
And say "It must be the weather",
But as we all have our stories, there is always
The import of the weather.

Elizabeth, January 25, 2008
Early morning, throughout the day—

44

When by the while, as hours close through
The night, there is a sweet peace,
Before, and, that left, afterward.
The baglady sinks into her own final,
Miserable oblivion, as the careful infant turns
On his comfortable back;
Exhausted lovers find their quieting,
And the fieldhand's muscles soften,
With permission, for a moment's respite.
Perhaps more, or, then, less, the thoughtful
Awakens into the light of knowing inside the closing
Dark, and pleasantries with angst juxtapose
In engrossing fashion, to fence around the joy of
Consciousness and the foretelling of more.
The larger questions, the quaint notions,
The teasing sensual all appear at hand,
But safely away.
Comes then, a time of flowing thought, awake
Or asleep, and it is caught, held a brief rambeau,
To pass into a day when just such reality is but a
Maiden's floral print, on the far side of the fence,
Within continuous droning of time past.

We all give up, we all accept,
To the rest of necessity,
But some reject what is a formless,
Soundless—colorless unknown that
Cannot matter.

Elizabeth, January 27, 2008, about
Six o'clock am—

The weather is cold through the balcony door
The balalaika is too beautifully sad—
The snow is so enchantingly cruel—

45

I hear dogs barking in the night,
The fartherest night, toward morning,
This January night of chill;
And I hear, to know, that I am nothing,
In this night of January chill,
Not even as animals,
Dogs barking their nonsensical songs.
I, anxiously, moving in ambivalence toward the only
Nothing that I can find—
Something, something real, full with beauty,
More a self in the vacillating stances I enter,
But within which I impotently move,
This January night of chill—
The balcony door just open, so that I know my
Thoughts are without rhyme, rhythm or
Sensibilities which would, if with a spark,
A cord, an ember, cause all to somehow
Come into being; and I would flow, a flow toward
Something, somewhere, some of those
Constructs I lost along the way.

Silence forms a kind of rondo, for it is without sound,
The music and whispers of the dead,
A reality more than the useless wrestling before.

Elizabeth, in deepest night,
January 29, 2008

Princess, "Queenie" that I have been declared,
I would like, please, geranium tea,
Wetted scarlet and pungently sweet,
And flowing about as clouded skyboats,
Shimmering whiteness here and about,
In hues of wandering childhood blue—
Will to grant fuchsia ruffles in great abundance, centered
With a profusion of crimson rose silk,
Draped as new blossoms,
Falling down onto the gold on which I sit.
And to the
South,
Grant to me, a chartreuse meadow with
Smallest medieval beasts, playful and picturesque
As much in fancy as silent paintings.
And then, when these are gathered to me,
Place, if circumstance be in all acceptance,
My crown, it by the hand of him whom I found with
The eye of my heart, the hand of my peace.

Elizabeth, January 30, 2008
In deepest night
Home—
A fanciful desert of words to
Celebrate—

47

Coming to first awareness was the flight of wild
Geese through my south woods, in spring
And summer, last, continuing into
Now, this following February morning,
Their non-melodious barkings, at the first,
Were offensive, but they were brief, distant,
And have remained constant so that I presently
Feel, in familiarity and expectation, warmth at their
Morning excursions.
They have become known to me,
Non-threatening, accepting of my being, my space—
So strange—that in a cosmos of threat and change,
Too frequently shadowing its beauty,
That one can become comfortable with any
Singular entity which allows his thought, his being
As they are: a box, a vase, a bell—geese.
But there is, in the present, brevity, the distance,
If constancy, yet the unhappy circumstance of
Wielded barren.

I could not give of my accepting self to the geese,
That the distance not be—although I would give to any such
As my geese—sounds which would swell the heart,
And melt the eye; colors that would splash over all the
Pastoral, an embellished rainbow; fragrances
From the sweetness of flowers to flow over the
Hair of all women who love.
The box, the vase, the bell—the geese—
Yet, in the wisdom of natural law—these do not have
Hearts such as mine, spiritual radiance which
Must spill;
They can only benignly accept, affording in that

48

All the poor passion that could come to me.
Why has this grail been held from
Me, in its fullness; for in my beggar soul, I weep, into
The grail of part
Awareness, less fulfillment, with an agony
As words indescribable, that my geese
My box, my vase, my bell—these
Have no soul but appropriate
Silence.

Elizabeth, February 7, 2008

Images coming throughout the morning,
Saying my passion.

Raindrops are beginning to fall,
Slowly, quietly, as small
Unoffensive chatter,
Playing with the dry leaves—
Almost with apology in their reluctance;
These—like teardrops that will gradually
Lead to a flowing or sentiment
That is more wished kept in its capture.
For teardrops are the blood drops of the soul,
Painful in their leavetaking,
Hurting in their finding,
And so like the raindrops now, today,
In February chill—they should be seen
In their modesty, for they cover
Tendernesses
That ought be given homage,
And touched with, albeit metaphorically,
understanding.

Elizabeth, February 3, 2008
About 11:25 am
Super Bowl Sunday

Each raindrop, each teardrop, is itself,
Alone.

Clarity is not truly found in whether
There be the reality of a songbird,
A rainbow, a butterfly,
Or a mighty pine—
Any that our conjured semantics draw
And bind—but rather when all the descriptive
Necessities are taken away,
Only the left need among gifts,
Weaknesses and strengths that hold up
The guise of whatever beauty in whatever
Season—enters then the whole of the matter.
And if the leften be favorable,
It should be embraced, swept into the other
Inside chambers of such; if the leften be
Found unfavorable, beyond accepting,
A fully individual pre-requisite,
Then it should be placed away from the
Gathered inside chambers,
Either there behind, aside or away, to a place
Where it does not mist about its
Unfavorableness, to cause the gathered,
The spectator, the touching observer,
Or merely passerby to be troubled into loss
Of isness, being, in good need,
Gracious gifts.

Elizabeth, February 4, 2008
About 6:40 am

Thoughts—on hearing bird calls, geese barking in their
Flight in the south woods, all in springtime-like
Weather at faintest daybreak—

Camellias fancy my seeing their whole
Beauty, or so it seems, those of
Long ago, and those of a more recent
Season of briefest love.
They know no narrative attending their
Blossoming, and stand
Full pigmented in passion's
Sunset rouge: bud, offering, some into
Their full giving,
Others complete to the day,
Delightfully spent.
They call to me, from fartherest yesterday,
And closer yesterday,
But most in the absolute beauty of today;
I must gather and arrange, and to declare
The connecting camaraderie
Of the seasons, they each always entering,
Always departing, I will add small branches of
Cedar.
How small our worlds without beauty, if just the
Young, innocent harlot's rubied lips
Before defilement, or cherries hanging into
Complimenting before gathering from the summer warmth,
Yet the rose rose, eternal blush of tints of
Many hues, elegantly standing in summer's bliss,
But more, in the snow in the lady of the rare
Christmas rose.

Elizabeth, February 5, 2008

Noonhour time after gathering
Camellias—those very like Miss Buleah's,
Seen again in the camellia Richard and I planted
When we built here in the country,
It to first bloom in the season after his death—

52

The past must lie and it's farewelling,
And
The future stand in salutation,
But we are not to dwell in these environs,
But in the quickly passing
Cognizance of inner knowing
And it myriad manifestations,
In thought and behavior,
Brambled though often intrinsically,
Exquisically beautiful: the awareness of our being,
The fullness of the moment
Accomplished —
More in our hand than bread and fish.

Elizabeth,
February 8, 2008, about eight o'clock am

Beauty of sunshine in the outside cold,
Heralding the day, moment by moment—

We are, in morning's bright,
Very angels dancing true,
Gods and goddesses, leaning on our ease
Into the glory of the new gold.
There is the excitement of promise,
Expectation, the thoughtful teasing
Of the unknown;
And dewdrops are surely diamonds,
And winds silvered breath.
And with energy impeded by joy and hope,
Steps are quick and purposeful
Until the golden eye has found its
Zenith,
And with apology, cannot hold it.
Westward dim, though yet far distant,
Pours little drops of vinegar
Into our glowing, amorous jasmine tea,
On cloths of nasturtium hues—
A small and quietening shadow with
Each portion.
Angels pause often now, and we gods
And our ladies sigh on our arms, for the hours
Quickly come together and the magic of
Firstness, innocence, naiveté, dreams and
Remembered fables slowly drift with his majesty
Of light into the rest and impotence of finishing.
Morning glory—when awareness awakens us:
Come, come—but more, linger into ever.

Elizabeth February 11, 2008
Early morning mania

I reached for my writing pad, after an attempt to lift
The small glow of light from the candle, off
The rug, thinking it a fallen tissue.
What most absorbed my attention was a growing melancholy
that
Was in descent, full upon me—in my silence—
That the details of my paintings were slowly
Wandering into the growing shadows and dark.
Such happens routinely, but not so that we are aware,
In close proximity, and in a matter of
Short hours.
The vibrant colors, the defining lines bringing pleasant
Forms—indeed the subjects chosen—
Came through hours of my fullest and best energy;
Now, for a space, a moment forgotten, they
Will be silent, a non-reality.
And I am in place again, overmuch of a circumstance
Ordinaire, for the day and night are certain,
And the flaying of violent spring storms not
Uncommon.
Still, to be alone with myself, with my toys, alone, in
Wind and dark rain—to see my pieces slip away
From their radiance my joy has brought, to the
Shadow of the inward eye—awakens metaphorical imaginings
And discoveries.
I will pull the robe that is heavy around the lighter one,
To sleep into new light. My thoughts are an absurd
Pantomime, and will fly away, not to matter,
They, or their fullest being—they never did, do not now—

They never will; I am merely a detail that will fade into
Shadow with the arrival of the appropriate
Circumstance.

Elizabeth, February 12, 2008
Transcribed about 10:00 pm, having been composed
Just after the noontime storm, with electricity
Being interrupted through twilight intervening—

In the flowing, pulsating blue and lavender colors,
I found myself, I thought, perhaps to be
Dying.
I sat mesmerized, close to being transported to,
Transmuted into, somewhere,
Something, blue and lavender hues into a
Flowing still—so by the tinted light and its
Movement around my troubled thought.
I am afraid, and I know little to dispel the fear.
There is no certainty, yet it is always the
One meat and drink to our souls' wish.
Will the blues and lavenders pull me into them,
And will I be stepped over to the other side where
Certainty surely is—or, perhaps, not, as familiar
Wisdoms cloud even this comforting surmise:
The character of Moby Dick—blue-white, good or
Evil fire; the heavens upward blue into endless
White,
Lost oblivion; the sea, deep blue into depths of complete
Dark:
With angst and shadowed reason, the certainty
Wish, still.

Elizabeth, February 14, 2008, about five o'clock pm,

After looking intently into the computer visualizer,
Eliciting pounding thoughts—

57

And he did lie with her,
And
She with him,
And they, together, did deeply love;
The hours hung, a generous
Season,
And danced away with quickened step.
Her earrings haloed as their
Bands, and out their lips
Was written their sounded
Troth.
Record cannot script their narrative
For it flowed as golden mead between them,
Into an histoire found only
Within their spirits.

Chocolate and mimosa, ancient oils in
Hidden Persian jars
Decorate this knowing.

Elizabeth, February 17, 2008

About nine o'clock am, up since
One thirty o'clock am: fatigued with thought—

Spring

The lifting of a prayer,
The paradise of a morning meadow;
The blade of striking pain,
The release of a giving smile:
Such finds our days against a sea
Of blue not quite to be captured by the hand,
And the sky, vast maiden waiting beside.

We enter and gather, to, on our beds,
In questioning dark, ponder—
Such is our universe of being,
Lying just next to the universe that
Houses all—and the sound of silence,
The ever amen.

In the night all properties lose their particulars,
And we are left naked before our inward eye,
To question the reason in being, other than
To know love and beauty alongside their shadows.

The song of the turtle dove under the distant
Morning star,
These with props of graceful forsythia and daffodils—
All quite in thought in night's wash of dark—but still
The heart quickens to another bleeding out of
A season of birth, of promise and reality,
The steps that write our humble histories.

Elizabeth, in deepest night, 3:40 am
Truly real, but more, remembered
Early spring night sounds: Roman thoughts—
March 1, 2008

60

Dead crimson is, without comparison, exquisite,
Faded rose its close, most laudable
Companion;
Washed blues into white speak
Peace and Madonna serenity;
And closing flame shouts in purist hues
Conclusion into twilight, dark,
And tranquility.
This palette reveals the way of all flesh
And blesses the hours of the
Pigments' brightest faces.
They are not record of regret, but a sign
That life is an exercise in a
Progressive varieting of beauty,
Emergence and glory into the wisdom
Of conclusion so that the cycle
May be continuous,
A constant in domains of presenting
Unpleasant change.

Elizabeth, March 1, 2008
Three-thirty pm
After viewing blossoms in their decline,
Having been beautiful when gathered,
But in their closing, now superior,
To my eye—

And our space is that of a thousand
First, white gardenias, in gentle warmth,
Their glow turned golden and
Reflected in the ever jewel
Of heavenly waters,
Our time of moments gathered closely
Together in these as the reflection
Makes its exemplary path from the
Eastern bright to the waiting
Western dim.
We are in being, catching our moments—
These as raindrops, small universes
Within, holding our loves and wisdoms,
Our purposeful and idle steps, the
Passions in our souls,
The resting when we are spent;
And then we are in absence, more now in
Dream and fable, history embellished,
Sentiment buoying up past our
Holding—
That we did, and well, walk these
Golden, earthly sands.

Giving and requiring, seasons pour out and allow to
Lie, these sands, our houses for our very
Breath and life which hold the seed of soul,
Even over into eternity:
A vapor, a sigh, a shadow, a whisper—an apparition
Of some worthy and beautiful, or unworthy, but with
Beauty—yet, still, substance that was.

Elizabeth, on pond of early spring morning,
March 1, 2008, the peace of promise,
The angst of holding—about nine o'clock—

I wait the moments which will, together,
Become the deep night hours.
I watch the small, variegating light,
And hear the unmeasured silence,
My thoughts within it.
Is this the peace I wished so for,
In the time of battles' fiercest,
Or is it the left-over breath of life
Already given.
Time is an elixir to experience which
Renders sentiment washed through so that
All is as it never was except in
Worded or written record;
The heart has with the mixture run its distance so
That now I have neither yesterday or today,
And tomorrow, a photograph to be
Filled, to fade as has the heretofore,
Now simply, whole.

Elizabeth, March 2, 2008

Twilight into early evening,
And
The true reality of nothing—

All matter has left me,
For I have lost myself from it;
Touch and voice, chambered spirit—
These, but for the innocence of the natural,
Are perished in my thought.
None care, nor can be in truth,
A circumstance I stand in as well,
And so in early morning resignation,
I bend.
I will rise again, and walk among my fellows;
Activities will commence and those
Unknowing, those that fatten the path of
Our steps,
They will laugh and plan and know
Lostness as a social statement.
But I will be among them, a spectator apart
To my passion, standing, but more bent than
Before the early light which haloed my
Recognition.

Elizabeth, March 5, 2008, 6:10 am
Hard realization—

The candle's flame is beautiful memory
Of passion spent; it's left, cold and unfashioned
Residue is reality.

In assurance blessed, the bramble
Is, in truth, my newborn
Meadow;
In the knot lies my apple, radiant;
The falling twilight hangs rarest silk,
And the moonglow in dark
Speaks satin ribbon flowing out.
Proclaiming are these then:
There is enough in bitter flesh
To find love of it, and so I
Continue to eat my heart,
Starlight, the butterfly's gold just
A perception above.

Elizabeth, March 6, 2008, about five o'clock
In the morning—
After Steven Crane's verse

65

Reminders of losses appear and run away,
On the sentiments of melodies,
Colors, and fragrance,
In thoughts of yesterday.
They are at once heavy and staid, to
Become ephemeral, lifting away,
Forgiving their oppressive taking.
But we are become fuller in our losses,
Most so when we record and ledger, to find
Bounty of good left;
And then when they have appeared and taken their
Leave, as our awareness arranges,
We keep, in the vessel where our passions,
Both pale and bold,
Reign, our tears as silver pearls, memorials
Fleetingly beautiful, to our lost parts,
Grateful for what was, and, more, what is left,
That which is, to be clasped, and held,
And felt, for its season.

The night is not forever.

Elizabeth, March 8, 2008, throughout the day—

Acceptance spilling over—in growing awareness of
Any alternative, save the complexion
I bring to it—

66

Gold does not press me,
Save in lack with need, or in the
World of senses,
But rather the fullest knowing in a smile, lost, as failing
The bringing of the flower to be kept
Its colors perpetual,
Riding ever the carriage of the canvas;
Or almost more, giving over to idle thought
The poignant motif of the splendid
Concerto, in its quickly passing.
This recognition of alternate gold gives
To me, in this moment,
A contentment, for it waits, again, for me,
Not to be earned, or discovered,
To be finessed or taken, but openly,
Freely received.

Poor indeed, am I, when my purse is
Empty of these. I realize, though, that many
Do not share my reality and the losses
Are not losses to them,
Only to me for them.

In my petaled, wind-washed, moon and
Sunlit reality, I am deficient beside overfilled.

Elizabeth, March 12, 2008, 5:55 am,
Having risen at about 3:00 am after good, short
Sleep—

In time past, I have cursed the afterwards,
The beginning of the wait until
The next time;
Now, the complexion of my thought
Has taken on blush to its ashened hue,
And I lie on my bed with contented
Thought of what has been,
Even into conclusion,
For reflection is like soft whispers
Blown over quietened coals,
That they gently rise to radiance again,
Without any expectation of
Remaining in fullest strength,
But lingering into the great hall of
Memory, softly,
Where they are never lost.

Elizabeth, March 12, 2008

6:35 am, feeling content
Even yet, in losses—

And I will take the red of many teapots,
Those appearing along my chambre's ceiling,
To paint them filled with the dreams
Of a young girl, of quest and love,
Of capture and the sensual prize
Of the first hours of lost innocence
When purity is bested by waited,
Long, of holy birthright's
Gift.
A fragrance will accompany her thought,
A wash of faintest rosegold,
A very cloud of flowermist, and these
Will come in floating paths of the light of
Midnight's smile,
When the magic of the unseen can work
Its select maneuvers.
The romance of thought is as beautiful
As first wish and touch, the strength of new
Silkened thread, and the foundationing for the
House of untainted pleasure out which
We yearn in the routine of mundane reality.
Blessed be the good fatigue of nearby sleep,
Of passing freely among the levels of
Awareness our thought affords;
The beauty it anoints is fairer, and more
Desirable, than any, save the
Recognition of new, first day,
In the season of beginnings.

Elizabeth, March 14, 2008, 1:15 am

An image which appeared as I roused from sleep,
To fall back, and thoughts that ran to meet it,
So that I must to pen—

Morning Notes, March 18, 2008

I know that I barely keep illness at the edge of my being; at first Consciousness, I am sure that some presence is in the house, or else I assess the circumstance of there being or not—who is left to be. To be alone is to be without definition, and some may choose such, but I think them cowardly—finding peace by merging with the infinite, efiteness at its best, or worse. Rather we are created separate parts, to then extend, individually, and enjoy peace as the Greater whole.

When I am pressed, I am usually within the exercise of inventory, At night, and I wish to go out—I feel that I must—and gather flowers: beauty I cannot see, but knowing it, alone sustains me, with form, and without, most needed when the world shadows its form, the night metaphorically that circumstance.

And fears of storms—those of thought and those of winds in trees and clouds, for they take away the fruits of time, yesterday becoming the pretender to everything.

The subject of men is always with me, although I do not always want them with me, but they comprise a woman's greatest expectancy, no matter the difficulties included. They are strength within their pain, they offer the truest compliment. I think we sometime offer their burdens to us to embellish our own worth at bearing them—like listening for Daddy's steps at mealtime, from the field, or Richard's arrival home at six o'clock—no matter the effort in meal preparation, no matter how heinous the drunkened nights.

That these thoughts dance in my reason and lead to silent conversations which offer up insights to living leaves me alone

70

again, for others do not care to think on these matters, or at least to entertain with full awareness.

There is more to bipolar illness than mood—there is intensity of thought extension—and it can go all the way out to confusion. The care for whole truth is insistent beside allowing all to simply be; this is my daily struggle and the study of seekers, redeemers, holy men, written truths, and such intrigue me until a study is completed; I count my jewels gained only to hold them silently and resume my walk which does not acknowledge them, and they lie fallow until rare instances call out their light.

How small our great cosems, bounded on all sides by conclusion and our many maneuvers to placate our such knowings.

The moment is a difficult construct: it offers the entire beside damnation.

How much delight in my aloneness—how much pain I know in its reality.

The weather is early spring balm, like the mood of the couple in Arnold's "Dover Beach"—

How much, how much—if only . . .

Elizabeth, March 18, 2008
Thought, wandering and wondering,
Mid-morning—

On Forgiveness

Forgiveness is simply the lessening of a deep response to a hurtful circumstance, made possible by the passing of time and intervening activities, thought, and feeling. In that fashion, is our giving up of first sentiments and remembering. The personality of the individual and the strength of the incident and response are contributing factors; most fall within the same middle.

I cannot hurt more, again, than I have already, other than in brief, staccato moments, as thought and will allow. Left only are repeated playings of what has already been.

Dislike and hate, prejudice, spite and incompatible sensibilities do not matter, only the managing of thought; for all hurt is loss of peace, and the words of Cicero ring true: "There is no loss that time does not lessen and soften."

Remembering—the mirror to time
Past,
Yesterday, manifest—

All is a tender bramble of flowing thought.

A God Presence is in us,
Individually, personally, particularly,
As in the blossom,
The golden beetle and the
Star,
The single blade of grass.
We are together in our each separate
Relationship, forming individual and
Collective means
Of expressing
Dependence and devotion.

Elizabeth,
March 21, 2008
Good Friday—
Begun about four o'clock am, continuing
Until about eight o'clock am—

Thoughts, thoughts,
Companion to "On Forgiveness"—

It has been Easter: please, please let me not
Lose myself in yesterday thought—
So far back—or in thought of today—
Of what—save beauty in solitude where my
Thought meets its beginning portions
And in the present is rendered confusion.
What is, and what is not: in our
Hearts waits the answer, but we all wish
Not to know, and push aside to reach
For our various dolls,
For the moments that follow,
Even a pause of peace.
It is the long way which requires, and to
Bring to it, we search hourly for
A suitable fare.
Oh Face, now draped in darkness,
Bare your heart to your own, that the night
Pass with swiftness, our gathering little buds of
Wisdom as we quickly step,
So that we know a day divided from truths
That bend,
Those such as yesterday's which teach
The revealing lessons.

Elizabeth
Easter Day, March 23, 2008

Spent alone with conversations with
Only faithful Michaela—

74

The cello wounds,
As does the silence into
Which it falls—
And yet, the myriad voices of memory.
I am in a ditch of sounding
And unsounding desolation;
Would a Samaritan come,
Could I be bound up
And healed.

Elizabeth
Reviewing the day, Easter Day,
March 23, 2008

Alone—

75

Only gold is gold, and only in knowing
Is life, thought gold, word
Gold, embellished by sense
And touch golds.
And these are the moment wombed,
Dressed with the dreams
And fancies of yesterdays and tomorrows,
To push into still others
Such, but with the wisdom that the
Birth of new knowing, new truth, new gold
Is out the moment only,
These to congregate into our
Seasons:
Old death, new seed, pomegranate blush
Inside a thousand white gardenias,
Toward the hickory in sunlight,
Very glow through its leaves, into
Chill touching the full cheek of the
Crimsoned hollyberry—and new death,
To lie until old death, a memory, to become
A new life of knowing,
Celestial gold in moments chained,
To become part of the
Eternal circle.

Elizabeth: thoughts in deepest night,
March 24, 2008, 4:50 am

While painting the hickory in Autumn gold
From memory for the cover of
My smaller book of verse,
Hopefully to be published by summer—

I saw it in the shyful shadow of the
Hanging drape;
I saw it in the quiet corner where my olive,
Papier-mâché catbird sits;
I saw it in the deeply hued centers of the coral
Lilies in their painting's capture; I saw it in the early afternoon halo
Of the standing lamp;
And I heard it in the pirating forgetting as I
Slipped from one level of consciousness
To another, one of peace—until
Awareness abruptly arrived; and then
I heard it from small buds into full blown
Blossoms sounding wisdom and
Accompanying words of its guarding
Lieutenants; indeed, I heard it in the entire
Span of the garden of my thought.
Not to be escaped, the morning has stepped by,
As dew lifting away on sunbeams
Now moved into their lord's round,
Towardward, to the westward dim.
And left is the promising and impotent
Afternoon, prelude to twilight and coming
Dark.
We hold no moment, but imbibe freely,
In the masterful half-smile
Of the reality of tense.

Elizabeth, March 26, 2008
Early afternoon fatigued after busy, fruitful morning,
Counting the time left in the day,
Before entering, once again, the
"little death"—

In Sabbath quiet and stillness,
Within a grave now greening with new
Seasonal beginnings,
The orchestration of the strings of my heart
And the gentle menagerie of nature's voices gave up
A medicinal potion of such great
Strength that I cast aside
My wayfarer's tired cloth to don
Vestments of worship and peaceful wholeness.
It will not stay except in its residual
Strength, the smile of full lips,
The constancy of rainbow colors;
The opal's fire in friendly light,
The towardward of all steps;
In these, each, is the staid and balanced, the
Fountainhead of all returning beauty
And promise,
Providing the happy press for the swan who
Glides patiently, in loveliness,
Into Avalon.

Elizabeth, March 30, 2008
About 10:00 am

Absolutely full beauty of the season outside,
Pushing into—

So little is that real, and for only the
Space of its recognition;
Yesterday is merely yearning of sentiment—
It was, but it is not more.
And it can not ever be more than the echo,
The shadow, the whisper, the sigh.
Colors, sounds, the arranging of the
Early evening—all will be of reason
Or emotion, words of dressing for the place
Of farewelling, reality slipped
Away into the great collection of all.
Intensely pleasing parfumes, winter's
Woodfire's smoke, the concerto's
Poignant motif, passing,
Instruct the more often unacknowledged
Lesson of mortality.
All that we know, have known ever, good,
Splendid, fair—they are apparitions sweet to the
Passing thought, and nothing of anything
Can be held;
It can be recorded and wept over, esteemed or
Rejected, but its reality is a passing
Circumstance, and we are, in this day's history,
Weary with our reachings to hold.

Ah, Sleeping Beauty—more, beautiful sleep.
I believe the hound has finally won the chase.
Elizabeth, April 2, 2008, eventide

The night is long, an exhausting work,
Thoughts abounding in the silence, loudly
Touting their reflections, accusations,
Remembered trivia assuming
Oversized proportions in the absence
Of light.
And the good known is wept over,
Its largess drawn by the lines of its absence,
The conjured place of its
Dwelling in the uncharted dark.
Can life of the day truly extend into the night.
It cannot know the freedom of thought
That the moon pours over,
Stars touching awarenesses that are held
In the great hall of convention in
Day.
In night, we not only know again, and more,
Ourselves, our truths and firmly
Held, unexpressible postulates,
But we also lose the draught of light which
Allows the endeavors of what we conclude to
Be of our true hearts.
Conclusion of a portion of self arrives on the
Wings of the self that dreams,
Mourns, remembers, and questions.
Night is long, its fare dear, and when the
Morning breaks, the new blossom is larger,

Fresher, more to give to the day;
And sometimes it is smaller, and weary,
Able to only give over to the
Unrelenting light of the requiring good.

Elizabeth, April 4, 2008, 9:00 am
Morning after night of two hours sleep,
Fatigued, but with the gold of productivity,
Yet weary to greet the day—Richard's sixty-fifth birthday

I am touched in a fashion, faery-like, by the
Sound of silence, in this time after
April's storm, lying in eerie, struggling light,
Counting the unnumbered
Sandgrain bells, ringing, ringing,
In their continuing fall into my hearing,
Collectively effecting sound out the vast
Nothingness.
And the absent image, moving about,
Here in the dim, there in the shadow, close in
My multicolored, multipeiced imaginings.
No sentiment left, my thought is empty of
Togetherness, of prompted silent
Conversations, full with unfelt touch.
Emptinesses are instructive for they womb the
Embellishment of the ordinaire, and
Make exquisite the humble common.
Without is, contrawise, a full portion,
If unhappy, dressed in satin's brightened
Sharp loss, velvet's deep, close draping hurt,
And the loneliness of fine silk whose stories come
From afar, and speak of love,
Left crumpled, at the foot of the bed.
Pour good wine over and perish these knowings
So that the sandgrain bells, the dim
Roomscape, my leften heart will not bend
To this time of bare, not to be made full
Again with such as the spring storm.

I cannot see the colors of the flowers, passion
Held from me, leaving me a vial

Unpoured, a petaled throat unviewed,
Fancies dying in their unacknowledgement.

Elizabeth, after the storm, alone and reflective,
Hunger and needs deep within—
April 4, 2008, just after noon—Richard's sixty-fifth birthday

What has happened to my sweet time:
The fresh breath of morning falling about the new
Baptism of meadows and glens, of roads
And lanes; the friendly counterpointed
Orchestration of the menagerie of
Woodlands and distant dreams.
Can my words, my raindrops and rainbows,
The sky spreading gold,
Petaled glory under whitest clouds
Against piercing blue—and early moments
Of promise—can these words not now fall onto
The silken cloth of record.
Perhaps is lost the beading, the jewels of fabric
And leather, the hewning of cherry,
The musk of the splendid equine beast —
More, the fruit of the earth and hearthwarmth,
The binding of camaraderie, first passion and
Its overfull afterwards, good honor and reverent
Awe—
These have departed from my palette, my pen. Could these
Have, like that taken by the handsome, agile
Highwayman, have been gathered away
In his night, and now all left is the night for these
Is no substance to what would be day.
Ah flame, let me be your moth; leap higher that
You embrace me who loves your beauty
That is such that it quietens into peace.
Let temple bells of forest trees in wind-charioted smoke
Ring out the song of the mourning dove,
As beauty of flame and flesh marry into one,
For I am weary, and wish the companion of
Nothing.

Elizabeth, April 9, 2008, about nine o'clock am
Great despondency and emptiness,
Realizing the gravity of my words—

84

Wet chartreuse and polished lime,
Behind and to the side,
Stood, canvas to blinking browns
With bright touching of yellows and reds,
Darting here and about
While winds floated like peace rolling out the day.
The magic of springtime knows
No bounds, or fully telling description,
Except in our hearts,
Our senses wedding with their source,
Their very Alpha, the Presence
We call "Devine."

Words, the entire matter of semantics,
Is so much the lesser carriage—
More the image with fancied colors; the
Thought, in feeling, not words,
Gives forth our most devout
Praise, with thanksgivings.
Andso, it is in silence that we communicate,
Merge into the Holy,
And words fall as afterthought.

Elizabeth, April 10, 2008
Notes to accompany the piece of
Daddy's wild honeysuckle—

In early breakfast matins, simple, familiar
Industries calling out,
A sweet ambiance fell about,
One of love and deep sorrow.
Weeping out its finishing fragrance, stood
Daddy's gift of years past,
Wild, pink honeysuckle, taken from his creekbank,
Gifted gently to me.
Within the shadow of a thousand while gardenias
Lifted this botanical prayer, of presence
And care, of yesterday and the moment
Passing in a kind of glory.
Shadowed, whispered, breathed was He to me;
All that was before became again, and with it,
The pain of loss, the boon of holding,
Rare paradoxical circumstance that marries
With my heart daily, so wealthy
Are our days.

Elizabeth, April 10, 2008
Early morning, seven o'clockish

On entering the kitchen and breakfast room—
Daddy's honeysuckle's dying fragrance
Wrapping close around me,
Their gathering two days earlier—

In the knowing shadow of the between
Of consciousnesses, I knew a brother had
Murdered his sister,
To allow her to lie, in her green shroud,
Awake in her sleep,
Living pain her emptiness of the severance.
Like a cloud floating in its blue,
As receiving morning golds after dark,
And drinking in successive seasons,
Their old, new sweet nectar,
While walking in the silence of such as stars
In merged, still assemblage,
He tears flesh of flesh, and rebukes the
Womb-bed they journeyed out;
And in it all, in pathos too great for her,
Even in death awake, he moves
Unaware.

Elizabeth
An image with words, phrases which came
On waking in early evening;
No thought of Wayne of late—just the
Always there—the full hurting loss—
Today, April 12, 2008, about six years now
Since the incident that pushed
Toward the cementing of the schism—
Penned at about 10:00 pm

Slighting the old world theme of
Prosper Mérimée's novel, Colomba

Let me think, let me think—
Will there be, yet, another beginning,
For me to know—there is conclusion in these
Moments true, for I see the "little death"
Slighting the corners, breaking circles,
Shadowing all that was supposed to have increased
Today—but was there growth,
Increase—barrels and barns: no, not buds
Into blossoms or more variety of greens into upper
Canopies—not that I saw;
But only slow, movement from one thought to
Another—not to remember to do in steps,
But perfunctorily—images of beauty—
Grey, crumpled
Masses in graves of window squares, rounds of
Bowls and stems of slender vases.
The sun was cold, of April cold winds, and I
Searched out warmth within my rooms, in some
Yesterdays so filled with pieces of my
Heated passion, today left liquid flow of silent,
Formless color—"stranger"-like annoying,
In the color of encompassing grey.
And all in between just only sleep—listless stance,
Unreflective thought—sloth—yes and no—
Exhausted ease of will, stretching out to the all
Of oblivion—
And to myself left, a bit chagrin at the tease
Of loss, the splendid lying down to when
No purpose is imaged,
No responsibility of rising up—

Elizabeth, April 14, 2008
Penned about five o'clock pm,
After a "none" day, my mood way far
Down, hope only a construct—

88

When we sometimes, of gentle interruption,
Either in reverie or in an intense
Moment of sentiment, realize that much
Of life is shadowed, whispered,
Sung into a trunk, a flower box, a letter—
Or just the turning of the calendar—
We know, then, the deep hurt and joy of
Our mortality,
Its very failing and glory.
We cannot catch back yesterday or clasp to ourselves
Tomorrow, but in the moment, in chambers
Of the heart, in the various levels of conscious
Thought we know, again, in full knowledge
Of here and distance, confusing in the paradox,
But pressing closer in our eager hands;
And the dreamscape of tomorrow—a look
Backward with ideas of making straight the bent,
Bright the dark, sweet the bitter.
When vessels of life run over, we look,
Expectant and afraid,
But with sighs of longing, remembering
Strawberry wine, even yet, a thousand white
Gardenias,
Ours in the space as we draw breath,
A glorious resurrective phenomenon.

Elizabeth, April 17, 2008
Early rising, penned about 7:30 am

Somber thoughts, not yet for venture,
Thanksgiving underneath,
Nearly complete—

89

Time Is—

Time is now, when all is done—
The friendly sound of wheels lessening,
Voices and touch finding close, their own;
The sky at last colored dark,
Tender light closing its door,
And I, just me, unlike Cleopatra,
With pillows puffed up that I lie together with
Myself in my sport of thought.
Did a day process, with revelers and
Beasts, flowers turning their springtime
Hues into full radiance with the sun's newest
Smile.
Did there be day and life, expectancy,
Promise, dreams, giving and receiving.
How quickly the pall of night deafens the sound
Of day so that we turn hopefully,
Hurriedly toward the morrow.
Oh my heart, give me troth to every moment,
Not to be fickle, and clothed with infidelity,
To hold in sacred thought that I had
As comfort that I am.

Elizabeth, April 17, 2008, about 8:30 pm

Assessing the day, every day, now,
Promising my continued personhood—
Tenuous sometimes—
And no bell tolls nor do the little white and yellow
Saints stand in the wind—

90

Morningtime has settled in, early hours of its face,
Drifting down and about sometime in
The late night, into my present moments.
I know the glory that waits these fallen hours,
Time and time when night mysteries
Hush, and the day's promise is preparing—
Silent, certain promise: a benign reality, a beautiful
Fancy.
The season is, perhaps, the pentacle of the passing
Laid out in this calendar, the sun becoming more its
Full presence, without, yet, its heaviness;
Flowers stand and bow, his ladies,
A palette of glorious hues against
The lords of his court in majestic, almost
Spiritual-like ambiance, greens catching
The growing light in soft winds,
Becoming bejeweled, wealth to the eye,
A splendid holding in the heart.
In rising early, not to lose a single ray
Or image, I bathed with honey and bee soap,
And felt Mamma's gentle smile rise up
And over me. In several weeks now, red clover
Has bloomed, entering my windows, Jimmy,
Out the most distant chambers of my heart,
His presence speaking gently to me, joining, in his
First, words of my verse;—so long ago,
We began together, and he rests in far, removed
Yesterday.
Gardenias will not come for some time, now, but they
Will, to usher in the full radiance of summer, all one
Thousand of them, and their accompanying dreams,
Very beauty wandering my thought;

And in this lovely season of beginning and becoming,
I will greet each day with the joy of all the
Present, the bittersweet of all that past.

Elizabeth, April 20, 2008, About six o'clock am
Rising early, waiting light and knowing deep secrets—

Morningtime Afterthought . . .

I have said long of that
I feel in my deep,
But with the brevity, the suddenness
Of the striking blade,
I speak tenderly that my truest
Secret is that I love,
It assuring the entrance of purist
Beauty, reverend sweet.

Elizabeth afterthought
April 20, 2008

I am a wayfarer,
I have always wandered,
For I have been ever lost.
Where finds my hearth,
My porte, my sanctuary that
I may sit and ponder that fullness
Within my whole,
To know the true meaning of the
Path.

Elizabeth
April 20, 2008

My ever sentiment, when not
Engaged—and so—
As I lay me down—

93

Being and existing compose a dance macabre;
There is the lily, and there is the
Sparrow.
And there is the brook and there is the rock;
Laughter rings out as tears come into
Their claire,
But there is the oneness of each to
Always find a presence; and with them,
There is no realism in offering balance.

As night is consort to day, it stands regal
All hours, those of its own and
Those behind light,
The knowing of its ever-presence, its
Continuing press to become.

We step, then, and we laugh as we move,
Allthewhile in a lighted
Darkness before the brush paints
Out even shadows and whispers.
We dwell in the issue of good which must,
In a presence insistent, be scrolled back,
Leaving us to dance in place, at our own
Absurd pantomime that even the boon of scheduled
Light does not truly change.

Dark flowers, dark laughter, they feed and
Enjoin us to nothing with their
Dark fragrance and soundings.

Elizabeth
April 20, 2008, about nine o'clock pm
Dark, but resigned thoughts, for I enter another
"little death"—

94

The night was in its most silent deep.
And in a leap that is property of conscious
Thought alone,
I was awake with a desperate knowing.
The moon was down and a moan and wetted
Tears rushed their presence;
Before me passed my life, with all
The particulars omnisciently known,
An unimagined, mortal knowing that all before was
Now behind, and it of the color grey,
Despair of will and the appraisal of little left sand.
As quickly as it had appeared,
The epiphany, of clever daily covering,
Left its sentiment to the side,
And I rose immediately in a wretched effort
To somehow soften, to rout its truth,
If only with the oils of metaphor and symbol,
The wandering fragrance of hope
And insisting will—the press of a soul newly
Sighted in the face of challenged will,
These inside the understood tryst,
Which teaches most, perhaps, the natural,
The lesson of the drawn sword of determinism.

Elizabeth, April 26, 2008, at first light
A deep night's sudden, brief image,
More construct, that has been with me for
A week or more—these thoughts
Of a matron woman whose beauty and strength,
But not will, are failing: truly the
Circumstance of all my days, philosophically—

Were it not for the beauty of the moment, its
Constant memorials, the sword would strike, finally true.

95

I am thoughtful in these moments,
Those stolen from ritual and liturgy,
But as with the peace in unsung, early
Morning winds,
My plume offers its familiar joy.
And my thoughts companion the blossoms
I survey, in their glory, in hues
And patterns apart from the only real,
Their complexions, celestial.
They have arranged as to plan and circumstance,
As have our lives, our hearts—andso, I take
Jasmine in golden flow and add chrysanthemum
Lavender, rose rose of ancient love, its
Fragrance speaking;
Geranium blood scarlet with periwinkle's softened crimson
Against purist white arrange.
To glow and challenge the sun which will
Surely enter following the wetted painting of
Rain, I take and enfold marigold and sunflowers,
To take my blossoms, my thoughts out the sentiment
Of my kept heart, and sew a pillow
On which to lie where dreams may visit, bringing
Images sweet, as words tender, not to
Forget, but to dry into beauty, more, yet,
With the ephemeral quickly lost,
The continuing to abide.

Elizabeth, April 27, 2008, mid-morning

Stolen thoughts—Sunday morning, after
Gathering new blossoms, following rain—
Beauty extraordinaire,
Reminding of other beauty—

96

We are as thread in the lengthy fabric of time,
The wideness of its space.
We exist among complexities which
Cloud seeing: a bird in flight—
A rare jewel—a temple of extraordinary
Beauty, to become a mound of
Broken loveliness, more, sorrow as castaway.
How are we to know bliss in wanton
Peace when all we know is contrary to
And futile to the catching of a
Lasting peace.

Music, the butterfly, the first peach
Blossom—
These all pull out of us yearnings, even
Press, but the long days of
Summer—sounds, colors, forms fair and
Comely—always conclude, and to repeat,
Not to ever be truly caught back,
But to enter the great hall
We cannot even begin to understand,
But only ponder into fatigue
Or resignation.

How much a curse to must struggle

Elizabeth
April 27, 2008, early afternoon

Thoughts—

If I could hold a good feeling in my hand,
The moon's silver would dress my
Fingers,
The sun bracelet my wrist;
The stitches in my light, vintage cotton
Coverlet would sound words of love, happily
Sewed into it on a slowly passing,
Summer afternoon;
My first Coreopsis, very golden medallion
Of a king, would share its fragrance out its
Glory to my hair, and princess, I would stand;
And Daddy's English rose would fill my heart to
Bursting, with remembered industry of
Love and care.
A good feeling in my hand, I in my fiefdom,
Where colors and sunlight marry
Into wealth of a bride, the peace of
The white lily, the truth of worthy
Sonnets—
The beauty of the day has filled my hand,
And I am full of lovely sorrow,
To fly with the mourning dove away
Into a distance of echoes,
Where unimportant particulars fade gently
From thought.

Elizabeth, May 9, 2008

Thoughts in the early afternoon of a
Lovely spring day

In these moments, I know
The
Wideness of her
Aloneness;
She was left so much in
Needing,
And
I could not fill the
Expanse of her lack.
Could neither anyone other,
For we were both
Cursed with a lost part,
A separateness housed,
Yet with a continuous
Longing for that which we
Could not even
Understand.

Elizabeth, May 12, 2008

Thoughts of Mamma
In the late afternoon
Five o'clock pm

On Love

After all of the years, the words, the touches,
Love is like a grande parfume, intensely light and
Fresh, sweet as crushed petals,
In strength, as warm musk;
But in it, our senses marry, and we
Have a response, an experience, and it is
This contained all that we remember when it
Passes, lifting as angels' presence,
The sweet moving away of a Chopin
Nocturne.
Sweetness and hurting clasp each other and
We feel spirit-filled, royal that such
Has, in some part, been our fare.
Love is stronger than its description can
Attempt, but in its heaviness, it is good that
It farewells, for memory is comfortable,
Purer, safer, the baton to pass
Again into more riches.
Wealth in feeling is gold of many exchanges,
Tears adding the wet sheen and glow that are the essence
Of true romance.
Andso, we walk together, in love—walk past, into more
Than it could have been, holding.
The better way to secure is to let go, to allow
Loneliness cultivate feelings deep within the
Heart chambers that could not be
Realized othermore.
Our steps may not, most often, reflect this sentiment,
So much our penchant for the familiar, but the words are

More true, more capable of intensely beautiful being,
More than any of Cinderella, certainly not with a nose that
Suggests Pinocchio.

The irony is that now, always, some form of weak truth
Has taught that the meat of this knowing is accompanied
By the bitter sip of despondency.

The gifted wager, then—
Our gatherings—exquisite whispers of beauty to be become
Unsounded: issue out, in beauty and truth of fulfilling, and die
Into recollection.

Elizabeth May 13, 2008 about 5:45 am

Thoughts of loves past, the alone of now,
Their remembered beauty, the freedom and pain
In their passing—

I have awakened to the absolute of silence,
Of stillness, of dark, and it is, I think, where I need to be. The
entire circumstance allows the whole nothingness
Of existence to gather up, the essence
Of it, as being, to metamorphize easily to my awareness.
Curiosity almost enters, as I have ever questioned
The entire matter; for in the dark, there is
No beauty save the memory of the flame,
The passing of light, the embellished
Absence of sound. If it were not for our senses,
Would reason be the art that it is,
Since it can, alone, without sentiment,
Lead no where but back to itself—and with
The companionship to the senses,
Find that which gives meaning to a new moment.
Raindrops are hesitant, and the air is like
Autumn cool, on the front step of summer.
All is such a redundant exercise, saved from being
Castaway by its interweavings of beauty
That ever call to me; but in the dark is awareness,
Thought, and without a plate for the sensual,
It becomes a plateau of emptiness, nothingness,
Only ending to thought, and death to awareness.
So is the night, but more and more is the day.
A pall is drifting over me, leaving me
Away from others, even flowers and
Fragrance, the sweet bauble of yesterday
And memory: languishing, growing timorous,
Its gifts becoming lost to true knowing.
All is all that there is, here, then, in transitory
Likeness, away, away so that it truly,
In the long sleep of time, never away—

Like the Faulknerian guests at Miss Emily's Funeral.
I need to be where, what I know, because it
Releases the tension of expectancy and holding.

Elizabeth, In deepest night, May 15, 2008

How sweet the quiet
Of content,
That of holding,
Remembering,
Dreams and fancy,
Or,
Perhaps, most, the likeness
Of repose
In acceptance,
With the wealth of will
Left over.

Elizabeth

May 16, 2008
5:45 am

Light, whether quiet or awake, is my breath, and the wind, in its
variety of touchings, expresses, comprises my corpus.
Dewfall, early and late, is nourishing
Communion where it falls and ascends,
My physical and spiritual properties
Marrying together in my full person.
And the dark is the evening prayer to my fluid thought,
To the living, golden flow of idea and feeling.
The upward, vaulted blue in day and
Its silver of night is the most grande, the ultimate,
The superlative and immovable cathedral
With all the soundings lifting from below,
A congregational choir, sweeter than echoed whispers
And spented sighs;
Canopies of green evidence ongoing being,
And the presence of earth, in color and texture,
Speaks "Amen" to the Holy Visage of
Spirit, the purity of the sensual within the golden
Mead of soul, continuously: requiring necessity
Away—of crucifix or rosary, vestments or chalice,
For they are but beauty we humbly fashion,
Mirroring the very Face of the Only we can know and
Name, Holy Presence, now, ever, ever.

Into the night, petals are loosening, fragrances escaping, darkness
wandering into the soft mysteries of deepest hours.
There is an ambiance about—of losing the stitched
Coverlet of burdened cotton to the bright of flowing arieled,
butterfly silk with dragonfly luminance—day, oh day, your
Memory and promise are announcing your coming presence.

Elizabeth, in deepest night, May 18, 2008
Sunday morning after open house with Bobbye and Bill—
A close feeling in the night on early waking; God all
Around, outside, Holy Presence entering my awareness,
Inside—

His abundant ineptness, his deep
Unableness
Took my heart to him like a
Golden thread, with crimson castings,
And bound us together in a
Rainbowed knowing which would hold into a
Proper unraveling, and not a
Bramble to confuse.
For in his lack was the strength of
Humbleness, that my wisdom did not know,
But with will to stand with his
Known beauty, to rise out of it, speak
From it; and he made what was surely
A gentle proclamation that my
Knowing would instruct him into his yearning
Ableness.
The task was formidable but his spirit,
His soul placed just beside it, was eager to
Begin, to advance and hold, to replenish and
Continue, and I felt fully acknowledged
At the asking, hungry for the challenge,
Strong for the accomplishment.
Soul and spirit, out beautiful,
If innocent eyes, can bind good to all
Good.

Elizabeth, May 20, 2008

On the project of R.'s novel

I sat by the hearth on Sunday, last;
There was warmth with acceptance of a road too
Long to see its beginning.
Words, and smiles, unaware touches and
Narratives poured out like spring
Water in a hidden wood. There was no formality,
But a loose circle, as family around
A flame, the flame of long knowing, deepest
Sentiment of event and remembering.
Small flowers, small birds of happiness
Took our words and they sang a song of longtime,
Innocence, the ironic without bitterness,
Deep loss covered carefully with the
Learned wisdom of understanding, looked for
Like a priceless pearl.
And when the light began to fail, and the clock
Knowing its truth, we stood, embraced
With the coverlet of warmth that
Comes only from sitting at the
Hearth.

The buttermold was somehow lost, the heavy
Irons, heated in the day's embers,
Put aside with the flour barrel. The corsage
Of rosebuds and creekside violets, lying on a bed of
Feathered fern, remains vivid in color and detail,
Not lost as far, but these all together
Were as fluid gold pouring over
Us at the Sunday hearth hour,
It of the day's smoky dreams and
Faithfully come realities.
I think that although we can't go home again,

We truly can; the carriage may be a sigh, a whisper,
A fragrance, a touch. It may be felt only and
Not reasoned, but in the afterwards, we know that
Somewhere in ourselves we visited, briefly,
Moments, the touch of the angel's toe,
Lightly, upon these golden, earthly sands.

Elizabeth, May 25, 2008

A visit with Ruby and Jackie in Brookhaven—
Remembering, replenishing—
Our hearts fuller than the afternoon's
Red gold—

Light, light, day, oh day,
Brilliant circumstance of being:
In Thee manifests all that is,
And dreams and promises have
License to be.
If dark be, it is only prelude to more light,
A gentle nocturne wandering
Into its isness, its gold, though
Hidden, slowly emerging,
Breaking dawn,
The bride given in streaming silk
To her lord.
Trumpet and organ, hunt and feast,
Passion and resting—all house in Thee,
In light, the fullest, the only glory.

I leave the lamp in bloom, even when
I cannot see it, for it haloes
The scarlet and gold blossoms
Placed beneath it, beauty ever, seen,
And patient loveliness waiting the eye's
First capture.

My tryst with light, my scorning of dark—
Day, oh day, if Thou could always be,
Crushing every "little death."

A manic principle—
May 27, 2008, 11:00 pm
Eventful day, why to close—on, on,
Ever—
Elizabeth

109

Summer

First Musings in Deepest Night

Morning comes in, for me, like your bandaide smile,
The corners matching, in their closeting,
The deep pools of your eyes.
Morning comes on feathered hope of light,
Always in these moments, but Roman thoughts
Remain under the bandaide, the
Darkened centers of the pools.
I pen, thusly, for I remember as I feel,
And yesterday is more insistent than today,
At least in these moments of prologue.
Andso, I am full of anticipation,
Bounded by fear, for the eyes and smile have
Been in my thought, in my reason of the
Day, in my silent knowing, longtime.

Elizabeth, June 1, 2008, 5:30 am

Waiting day with the child's expectancy,
The matroned, seasoned
Pain of reality to be
Revisited—

ONE

Tenuous petunia, of faintest mauvish hue,
Geranium drying away Thy brilliant
Rose, and
Confederate jasmine, in Eastern flowings,
Blossoms only the breath of their
Fragrance, crinkling into ivory rounds—
Oh joy that Thou had'st been,
Gracing my rooms;
But weep, weep the way of beauty, to be,
To be, to offer then remembrance,
And follow the path of the grandest
Metaphors.
Even birds, the wind, the sky pale in
Your telling message, possibly
Because the heart is touched of sentiment
And it alive in much natural
Beauty manifestations.
If we could hold the thought inside the
Temporal—but in the way of all
Flesh, separation is press,
And we weep our tears into the largest
Urns.

Elizabeth

Across thought to verse ONE
To Michaela of night's conversation—
Untidy matters, beloved opportunities,
yet —

TWO

Sleep, sleep, sister to silent thought, very
Kingdoms of joy,
And beauty,
Waiting opening with new day—
Five-forty, early morning—
Near daybreak and the miracle
Finding into the circle
Again—
A piece, a curve, a portion,
Please, please, yes, please—

Out damned uncertainty
Within all certainty—just me, Elizabeth

THREE

In these moments, something fell—
It was the drape;
Something rose—
It was the day;
Something stirred with the
Candle's flame—
It was that behind the
Bandaide,
A softening,
Slightly, of the pools.

Elizabeth

FOUR

Chocolate and Mimosa,
Almond and the
Twinings of the grape—
Come to my thought,
To stay
Into
Image and bind me up once
Again.

Tired: 6:00 am,
June 1, 2008
New words, old thought—
As many as a thousand white
Gardenias—

Elizabeth

FIVE

And it is day!
Another "little death" crushed
Like rice paper under
Decorative flame—
So lost in form it never was
Until the wind finds
It and the dark
Re-appears—

Elizabeth
Daybreak, June 1, 2008

SIX

I slept a time to awaken with
Each visit of the
Blessed draught;
And with the waking came
A knowing of
Something wonderfully new
So that I came to feel
That happenchance was a faraway
Construct,
And that good was
Placed,
Long ago, to wash, at certain
Times, over us all.

I bathe in spirit, to dry away with
Coming knowings.

Elizabeth

In deepest night's reflection,
June 2, 2008

SEVEN

Holding close to me, then, I waited my father's flowers,
The sweet, purist Cape Jasmine;
They were not there the longest time, but
With the smile of coming summer,
Constant and widening, days and nights of
A confection's brew,
A morning unannounced, except for
Showing buds, found a very profusion of their
Ivory, fragrant wealth.
I gathered, and wept—oh wisdom's
Face, a heart's fullness,
Thou dids't come to me in years
And their fadings,
And not just days finding a season, but in
Lightings and shadowings of the
Heart.
Their glory made most my joy in the
Love they reflected,
Worthy the wait,
All the while in its patience of love.

Photographs, then, will capture visual
Radiance of that close inside, close and ever,
Growing in its recollection—other loves, my father and his
Entourage, its long progression of
Simplest, perfect
Beauty.

Elizabeth

EIGHT

So my distance to reflect—to view,
And hold, the most tender, most sensual
Touch, not tainted by unworthy,
Awkward conclusion, if only of my poor
Lacking, my most inept
Expectations of pleasure.
My thoughts, in mature roundings, truth of
Pain and freedom, of love and its
Many affectations—

In deepest night, June 3, 2008
After good, insightful,
If later brought,
Session with Dr. Norton; he takes up the
Glove of my one,
Most sensitive symptom, and does battle
Valiantly,
He, becoming, more and more,
Shadings of beautiful color
In the quest for truth.

Someday, perhaps, in the convoluted
Paths of the walk, as my
Silver—

Elizabeth

NINE

I did not ever want my father,
More than in complete approval,
But only his and my mother's
Happiness together,
For they were my well spring, my
Fountainhead, my
Pattern.
But in the long and intensely
Brambled course of our days, my pattern
Has never been a happy one.

Tender fodder—illness, poor models,
Inconsistent messages,
Absolute instruction—no latitude,
No room to move around
Without confusion and pain—

Bliss eludes after revealing; perhaps
The riddle is the most truth.

Elizabeth

TEN

Second Musings in Deepest Night

Ah, content in the morning's three o'clock,
Coffee of orange complexion,
And tea biscuits garnished with orange
Marmalade—
All within an ambiance of rose and lavender,
Lifting, of strings, the most sounding,
The haunting cello,
These inside dark, still,
My most constant, patient lover,
Whose arms wrap around the me that
Yearns for light only,
Offering caresses that I cannot but
Reach toward, in fickle hunger,
While a stargazer's bag of images, light made
Dark, contrast, loosing sensual touch—
These serving their songs—of life
And truth, of giving and receiving—of
Ultimately passion and resting, in thought,
In sensation, in spirit-filled drink of
Surely lonely gods and their ladies—apart—
But bound to the earth for a season.

Elizabeth
June 4, 2008, about five o'clock
In the early morning

Ebony can be made to smile when gold is
Quiet, most the heart that yearns for expressions
That wait, long time receiving;
Thirst prostitutes—

ONE

123

Ah, but to lie on flowered coverlets with
Pillows laced and embroidered, fallen about by
Old rose and lavender—
No one—no one in the house, less
The spectre presence in the low bedroom—
And in the dream of beautiful morn, Mamma died again—
Beautiful promise of glory which cannot
Hold, for the caught afternoon finds
Its place and we know dying glory to
Begin. Be vapors or climes,
Or soul out of its kept, joy laughs into a backward
Stance, and we are left with our hands
Stretched out, pulling from within our
Hearts, that the greatest courage does leave
Us, leave us with the alone.

Elizabeth, June 6, 2008, about nine o'clock pm

Very difficult day, everything off center—
Klimt, black paint, poor food in pantry—

TWO

124

Does being well offer peace or does
The in-between merely hold
The rose of hope of hours we call
Present.
To be confused and troubled within,
Of day and person,
Bright sunlight being used up as is to wander
Where angels lead, in chaos toward light and
Order of bells that ring, voices
That sing, and touches that heal.
Oh to be confounded, Swiftian
In idea and shut up in open, gaping
Wooden windows—moments caught that call
Out the tranquil that could not be
But for the forces that tear our thoughts
And impotent being.

Elizabeth, June 6, 2008, 9:15 pm

Alone with confusion—
Where is the ever, all away, away—
So close with the other side—

THREE

The sun was ever present, so bright
Today, yet in my rooms,
In my most inner chambers very
Distant like that September
Long ago,
And all the summer that passed before.
Thoughts are cruel, for they do not die—
But in the face of past
Circumstance,
Flourish again to wound and make to fall
Away.

Elizabeth
June 6, 2008,

Coming alone of deepest night when
Heart needs thought and they
Cannot reconcile but thrash
About together in skirmishes akin to
The hell of war—

Blue topaz, blue eyes, "Goodbye Sweetheart"—
And what of these—

FOUR

In the difficult and separate collection of long
Days and nighttimes, together,
In stillness of wanting, in silence of
Needing—
There came finally round to ledgering
And capture of self.
The French poppies she had sat among,
Very scarlet flow into virgin ivory,
With yet unbroken wing; the piercing
Demure of eyes whose petals had not
Yet closed; coming, shadowed
Feathered coat, still brilliant in whitest
Sunlit gold, her beak of perfect contour in
Elegant positioning—
These all had been, and been—
And to inward eyes would be always—
Through chill of season, through gifts and loss in
Circumstance, through loves taken in
Farewellings—
But now the dove is broken, and others
Will must fill the spaces of her sayings,
Those which were able with early morning bright;
Others will must to step in place in
Sunfilled lanes and paths, those which
Were comfortable joy to all—
For the dove is broken, bent and bent,
Reciprocal feeding, and innocent forgettings,
Looking past to other wished for frames,
Bending her feathers, so to the caesura—
That the wing lies, in quite surprised awareness,
On the earth, fallen, now, in a season
Abbreviated.
Some beings are so unlike all, or many

Others, so tender and fragile in
Knowing, that they struggle in their perceived
"somehow wrongness," providing
More estrangement to those others and,
Most, to self.
In that milieu, loneliness becomes the
Companion which perishes her in the turn.
Then so—
The golden, hanging pear in variegated
Symmetry falls free; the velvet Miranda-hued
Rose petal comes not to breathe
And loosens, to drift; the dewdrop rises in
The newest ray back to her lord,
Into the must away, and music of sighs and
Echoes grow silent in their unheard
Pining.
Thinking toward, at least first, conclusion,
Of Holderlin and his verse sentiments,
But with none to know either
Postulate: and so—
Save John

Elizabeth, in deepest night:
Words of hearted thoughts, intense truth
From courage not felt until
Now—
A memorable moment—
June 8, 2008, two-thirty of the early
Morning—
Full with the fragrant memory and
Reality of
A thousand white gardenias—

We all, Tennysonian babes,
In desperate rage of innocent
Misunderstanding or lack in it,
Beat out our music into an Assisi assent,
It ultimately lifting upward,
A joyful psalm of praise,
In consciousness of being,
Whatever its varied, purist hued
Complexion
Or pattern—

Elizabeth,
In deepest night,
June 10, 2008, 2:15 am

Esmeralda

Esmeralda is a lovely name, that of a
Lovely figure, but from a sad
Narrative—
So like the paths of days,
In and out,
Chronicling the saga of a principle
Played out called being, existence, living:
That wisdom brings certainty,
But, most, uncertainty;
Beauty, its reality in its loss,
And the pathos in love, perhaps the most
Gracious gift we find in our treasures.
Oh, the strength, the courage
To live, to love,
To excite in innocent industries,
And create and observe beauty.
Added only, left, is the joy in reflection
And remembrance,
The impetus to emulate all past
Glory.

Elizabeth, June 9, 2008, early morning,

Thoughts arriving at the hour of
Six o'clock—
Amid a thousand white gardenias,
Of my father, sun, and rainfall—
Benevolence indescribable—

In early summer warmth of the night's
True still,
The dark lifts its drape,
And the bud opens to her breast,
Fully hued and veined,
The color of still, its pervasive
Voice,
Trumpeting beside strings;
And the wind, its breath of touch,
Wanting, caring—
There is no more sensual or
Spiritual truth
To be gathered than in the fullest,
Truest meaning
Of this circumstance.

The mirrored reflection of Divinity—

Night musings, still—
Elizabeth, June 12, 2008, 2:30 am

My pen, my brush, my eyes and hands,
Governed by thought, conscious
And that deliciously unaware—
Oh universe opened to me,
As spreading dawn over all
Created—

Miracles and happenchance—
Nein—
Only our recognition in this moment—

131

Grey day, grey day, altogether, beginning
With the promise it was—
Not together, distant reflections swirling
About gardenias in their farewelling, purist
Ivory to tarnish and decay—but their fragrance
Most intense of the cycle,
Leaving us with their presence for another season.
Grey day, grey day, for seemingly there are
No buds, no thunder, nothing but
Ongoing heat until the earliest hours of morning.
Why to begin, why to finish—all will be forgotten—
The season simply embellishes the
Poignancy of the poor space of day.

Rose-veined figmeat, jeweled blossoms,
Multicolored, bright-cheeked berries, crimson
Into magenta, the unexpected reprieve of cooler
Winds—how to know fully, to hold, even
Into remembrance—all left is the knowing
That everything has been before, is, and passing now,
To be a chanson of quieted joy.

Not a good day—pensive dark lay
About my rooms, the sunlight like a prince
Dressed in gold with a schedule calling him—
Passing, passing—all will with the crocus go—
So difficult to close my hand around
The very moment that is, its breath wily vapors
Pulling me into unfortunate intoxication
Of futility, ennui's breath, heavy and covering.

Elizabeth, June 16, 2008
I forgot yesterday was Father's Day,
And today I remember that I forgot—musings of late Evening—

twilight time before deepest night
And the specters that ease into thought—

I feel as Jean Valjean, le Colonel Chalbert,
Le Monsieur who innocently
Picked up the small piece of string—
Trying to make reason, in their separate
Narratives, set the pear on its gold
Side with blush spread across—

Epilogue
To "Grey day, grey day"

Elizabeth
June 16, 2008

Hopelessly romantic moment,
A kissing ball of all my
Days, now
Separate from their care—

Elizabeth, in deepest night,
June 19, 2008
Just at midnight that will spread its
Dark rose over my pen and brush,
My needle, the pages of Bonhoeffer,
The hound of loneliness
That will inevitably catch me—

Saying goodbye is most often difficult,
At times abruptly, but always
As the fading of the rainbow, knowing
That it is there, soon not to be.
And to this season's gardenias, very much so, as
The closing of a beautiful song—
To hear, to visualize, and too dear to
Record except much like those
Of past such seasons.
One bouquet—for my love, one to flavor
The hearthroom, and one to grace
With beauty and gentle mood my little corner
Of simple industries.
The elegant, milk-white ivory of
Silkened suede, only accomplished by
Nature, has given over to tarnishing and deeper
Browntones, umbers and more,
Veins of earthtones.
Conversely, in the farewelling, the fragrance
Of these blossoms is that of a thousand
White gardenias, to stretch across
Another time of waiting for their special beauty,
And kept, sweet whispered complexion.
We cannot hold what is too beautiful to be,
But in spirit appears to part,
And so we must to glimpse and clasp to our
Hearts in their hurried passing.

Elizabeth, June 17, 2008, 10:30 am. Our passing
away of this special portion of summer, of my days, earlier and
now, today, this moment of true knowing—

135

Departed in hour of deepest night, but musings still,
Of that of nature—the brilliant sun in darkness away
To its covered grotto where it will wait its appearing,
As the moon at eventide —

The silence was quiet, at the least,
Without Southern qualities;
The shy moon neither spoke nor painted
And the wind breathed close to the earth:
A perfect moment for thought,
For being alone,
To delve into the hidden
Chambers of my heart.
But in this round of placidness,
This benign cosem,
I grew afraid, for sound is helpful
When sentiment bides in
Unstructured pastures.
Will I love, do I love—
Ah, lift and breathe heavily, Thou wind,
Speak out forcefully, O moon,
And paint with grandest strokes,
Silver and ebony against sleeping,
But remembered, lighted radiance;
And silence, unseen, roar, lion-hearted
And fierce—all Thee in chorus,
For in a quickly passing moment,
I did love,
And the moment died.

Elizabeth, in deepest night, June 20-21,
12:00 pm, am—the first day of another summer;
And yesterday, I saw a lone, remaining
Gardenia where there had been thousands
In white—so quickly, too quickly—
And so, why—

Beautiful Late Night Musings

Let me not fail to know the falling of one petal,
The passing of a single fragrance—

I did not love you at the first,
As I did not sense and feel with
Another,
But with your first feigned smile, the
Underside of the bandaide,
As the shadows behind another's eyes
Of piercing blue—only then did I know we
Were man and woman whose
Inner selves must come together.
I breathe in your inspiration as the
Constancy of another,
And I know in my broken self, but newly whole,
How much we all can be part the other—
To make music of laughter, as one
Has given me, sunshine, good days ever,
The fullest meaning of the gardenia,
Even he of a thousand white in early
Summer warmth:
Oh let me open and embrace, think and feel,
The paths of the bandaide, the glory
Of the gardenia.

Elizabeth, June 24, 2008, in deepest night
Of my loves who enlarge me,
Increasing the absolute feast of
Life—

And I slept again, this time to the
Morning's five and half circle;
And with awareness it almost caught
Again, a sob, the pain of
Unfinished fear.
But to surprised delight, I opened into
A wider consciousness,
A night of meadow, illumined of light,
Left over silver where children danced and
Played, running, skipping—their laughter
Playing out the music of this sphere of innocent
Bliss.
Orange married with chocolate to be plucked
From every green, and fancy drove
Our steps in beautiful happenchance—
That we were again as we were once,
From sea to can and be.
Tears misted with full consciousness, and the fancy left
Into the remaining dark.
My Mother's presence, inside my Father's
Shadow, was there, but not there,
And sweet but burdened with greatest sorrow,
I left, again, impotent to great indignities.

Elizabeth, June 29, 2008, upon waking—
I looked to the balcony and light was
Faintly promising—
Somehow, Friend, I had passed the night,
One of intermittent sleep, my draught, heavy—

In abject pain, I wander about in
Mists, and clouds, in shadows and whispers,
Sighs falling into.
Some flowers are too soft, too gentle,
Too beauty-clothed to bear the
Brilliant gold of the mighty sun king
Of a day.
And though they are of a kind of strength
In their loveliness,
They perish of their glory.

Elizabeth, June 29, 2008,
Seven-thirty am—

My solitude, and in it, among its various
Wealth, my loneliness is, in truth,
A celebration of self:
My unique camaraderie with nature,
My dialogue with my different levels of
Consciousness, my perception
Of my physical self,
Its beauty, and complex with simple functions—
These all are allowed me in the
Sunlight of day,
As many treasures as dewdrops in
Meadow, first regal glory—
Or in the intriguing road into dark and
Moonglow,
Silver pearls and diamonded stars draping my
Person and thought.
There is a kind of content, a placid space
When peace, as elusive as it is,
Can step out the shadows and touch my cheek,
As surely as a lover's kiss,
Full with passion of the coming rest
In contentment, very reaching home.

Elizabeth, July 4, 2008,
Early rising—about six o'clock,
Having risen at the two o'clock hour—

In the Night of
July 4, 2008, Two-thirty am

I awakened, and with a knowing, that of a
Ring of fire in my hand—
And it was bright, and it burned:
I knew that I was in a moment, that brief
Respite of not imaging, or reaching
To holding in flowing: and on the other side,
Losing.
We are, in the always, mostly present into
Having, or in the experience of holding, however
Brief—
Enough for the lost to be known and the wished for
To be engagingly close.
In reaching, there is press, a wonderful
Neurosis of isness, and in the clasping,
There becomes an almost nebulous blasé,
Awareness of the parameters of existence.
We, in an unkind moment of reality,
Perhaps not to even reach awareness, but intuition,
Know that
The heart is not really purple, but merely a legend within a Box, a
caught reaching of a Moment
When we walk again the plains of Carthage,
Lift Antigone's lifeless hand, and know
a king's beginning seeing, "This is the worst."
Andso, in a time that is metaphor to eternity,
We cease our reaching, but we do not yawn into the limberlost
That is about, where moths die

Beautifully in their destined flames—
And we search our purses—fare to find, the exchange to be, to
rise and—Of the bramble—see.

Elizabeth, in deepest night
Fording the river of damned ennui—

Where love and hope are tenuous—
Almost in the real, but academic instruction
That leaves us to truth: seeing, to
Reflect and die—
For of passion and resting there is truly only live
Passion and dead passion,
Both whose end is to be spent;
If the flower blooms again, is it, save beauty,
Wisdom to do so.

I will to my brush, at face of three o'clock,
For in it is a moment of reaching,
Holding, and losing,
But recording in color and form, images of
Beings—that we did walk these golden,
Earthly sands.

A pall, a drape, a mist, fair linen that
Somehow rises into the upward—
The glowing insects of conjured genius have
Given their hesitating light into the morn,
And twilight in early summer is passed another time.
An ecrued, lace pillow for my jaundiced
Foot, a lifeless, crimson periwinkle hanging
Into its sister geranium—
Both having served, to serve—
Into nothingness—
An Elizabeth afterthought to an epistle
Already said—

Much is gifted in little islands of
Quietude,
When the sun is not yet bold;
When figures do not move,
And birds have not heard their prompting
To early rituals.
Small thanksgivings wander about,
As memory affords sweet pleasantries;
Candles cast a mysterious shadow,
A matroned radiance,
Those together of dreams and whispers
Of beauty and good.
To speak to one's self, the heart
Of one's thought,
Leaving a sky of heaven,
An earth of seed,
And yesterday's touch, the birthright of
One anointed.

Elizabeth, July 5, 2008, about six o'clock am

Having risen at the three o'clock hour—
Putting chores to rout, finding softness that
Cushions the realities of the day:
Utterance of complete good will and content—

I think I have found some wellness beside my
Ever malaise—
Ah, to keep balance and a bit of grace
To the side—

All the House clocks Show ...

All the house clocks show the three o'clock hour;
The dark rose of midnight has bloomed,
And her petals now are joining
The remaining darkness to salute
And bow to coming day.
Thought which knows the promise of
New day is a glory that is blessing
At that moment into always, for a great
Part of yesterday we lose,
But a bounty we keep, to add, for
Embellishing, more, the present, the new day
That follows: a superlative in being
Not to be challenged.
And moments alone that allow this
Worded image is wealth to the hall of sentiment.
Night is becoming a good, a time of
Reflection with the distraction of my thought
Alone, this circumstance slowly becoming a chest
Of experience beautifully painful but
Concluding in a small grape of content.
The "little deaths" still require and are a dark
Journey in soul, but now, of recent
Time, as seed waiting, to burst forth in new
Green, joy in being.

Elizabeth, in deepest night,
Working toward re-assessment of what is
Metaphor to my entire cosem, knowing all the while
That moments will continue to visit which

Are like an enraged, arthritic hand,
Turned back on itself: but pain, like the
Night, is not forever,
Joy coming in the morning—

All the House Clocks Show . . .
Two

And so gracious is time that it stretches
Out the woundings that they become
Whispers, almost unheard, a morning
Mist lifting off the pasture into the
Untouching faraway.
I am happy that these words have been
Scripted, for my mood already
Knows movement, away into questioning
Beside acceptance:
To balance is, as in the remembered,
"always" difficult—
I cannot hold the moment—
But how fortunate that there is abundant
Beauty to restore.

Intensely I feel the trumpet and organ
Together, sunflower daisy in
Orange against scarlet geranium;
And when I walked out in the afternoon, last,
Following the spontaneous rain shower,
The earth smelled alive—
As when I was raven—
And I heard a melody from the
Mourning dove.

Elizabeth
July 7, 2008
Early morning

Thoughts Tonight, July Twelve
Faith

In fullest truth,
Thou, to my knowing, wandereth,
In Devinest, purposed steps,
Further and further from me, yet in that
Distance, in my soul's sensing and feeling,
Very closer than a prayer, a hymn,
Yet offering or sacrifice.
My need shadows over now my instruction,
And my reason is confused in a
Level above a widening content—
More like peace—
Arriving after struggle without trumpet and
Fanfare, angels and multi-glories,
And most, like a softly diffused stillness,
I more at ease in aware
Unawareness—

Thoughts Tonight . . .
Love

In the night, when thoughts return home,
I, in sweet musings, say "I will surely
Find him in the new day"—
So simple—
A hand's movement, a ring, a voice and
Handsome laughter—
Sunshine again, all again—

But in the new day, the movement is tenuous,
The ring unsounded, and no voice, sunshine away;
For distance, in many guises, and doubt,
With circumstance, are pirating our
Mutual care, our September passion,
Dressed in a thousand white gardenias.

Thoughts tonight . . .
Hope

Is it long until the end, or short—
Or perhaps is it long fear, of an end—
Or short, if we have, in good hours,
Cultivated our gardens.
Andso, there are seasons to remind,
Of that sentiment we keep;
In longest summerlude, there is good
Hope of longtime with autumn and
Harvest legends to be
Pondered.
But earlier than snowfall, sweetgum leafstars
Waltzing by unannounced, their color more yellow,
Promise a fuller, purist red, and we
Are pulled from our warm dream
To our questions,
Requiring, now, answers.
Wet and flower, fruit and seed, leaning
Into gold and shadow, dark and cold,
To, again, wet and green—
Hours and fears joust inside our breasts,
And we sigh into indecision, to reach for the
Leaf of the sun's smile—
And this non-occasional, covering masque,
This such madrigal will continue round
The hall of being until it cannot, anymore,
Be concepted.

Elizabeth, July 12, 2008 11:55 pm—

Others, This Morning
8:15 am, Monday

The sweetest melody rings out from my early
Morning balcony,
Feathers on the pale of coming day;
In fancy it is a berceuse,
Washed of all pain so that only the
Love of my mother's voice wakes me in these
Idyllic summer days of reminding warm crepe myrtle
And the rough and knarled hands
Whose touch smiles,
Speaking the gentleness of the love
In old England's gardens' rose.

Elizabeth,
July 18-19
Year not noted
Of my Mother and Father—

I embrace with gratitude the absolute glory
Of new day:
The grace of every leaf pattern,
Every glint of falling sunlight,
The maidenhood in these farewelling
Blossoms—
All become a coat of royal color and
Filling substance to my whole, my soul,
In delight and receiving bliss.
Even August, after rain, is a plentiful portion
Of the bounty of the face of Holy Presence;
Could joy manifest in form, angelic lines would
Dance upon my grounds, their voices
Playing my fingers as a master his
Instrument;
Only is now the moment, but the journey is
Filled up with these such beauty,
Alongside shadow and dark; there is, then,
No question to be pursed upon our
Lips: the leaf has both sides, but most in strength
Allowing the gold to announce new day
To lesser gods of true God.

Elizabeth, Sunday morning, 8:45,
August 3, 2008, after rainfall throughout
The night, a glorious prelude to coming autumn
And its rare beauty so that the radiance of summer
Becomes a beautiful dream, not ever lost,
But companion to other, ever beauty—

Let be first in my belly, warm bread,
First in my thought, all good;
Let be around about me full light,
And the soft fragrance of whole being—
Food and drink for beginning soul,
In the day appointed to us all,
We of slightest gold, we lesser gods.

Elizabeth, August 9, 2008,
About nine o'clock am,
Just after coffee, floating through sunlight
In a cosem of gentle, still melodies,
They of my dearest nephew, Jason,
Visited yesterday—

In these moments of content which seem to visit
More and more often, in deepest night,
I am struck with the complete joy of life; the
Darkness, the abject despair of past hours are
Almost unimaginable, and I am
Near to faint at the beauty about me: the hope and
Promise, the near gold of sunrise,
The fullness of day—
Its color, fragrance, breath, long roads
Down which to adventure; the softening of twilight,
The offering of quiet and rest of evening,
The gentle intruder of night that
Takes away on unhappy days, but opens
Out to the innermost soul on days
Of pleasant mind.
And the why of these climes is not, at this moment,
Important.
I have only one taint, one scar or mark
Of negative face: why did all of this beauty, this
Content, this sounding melody and flourish of color
Come so late.
I do not know, or even now, in most moments,
Care about the other side except that I do not know
That it will continue as this bliss I often
Now experience.
I am troubled to part it, or, in some circumstances
Fail to find completeness before the parting;
And in that instance I fall a portion from the contented ease now
Of my filled heart.
The fullness of touch, and voice,
The complete of felt care,
The absolute holiness of the face of nature bear

Me up in these moments,
And I am comforted, perhaps more, instructed, that all
Before was a requiring prelude,
Necessary to now, though seemingly long and
Painful, overmuch;
But the "now", arriving in unexpected moments,
Could be the flower, the bejeweled spirit belt,
Finally unclasped,
Offering the fuller bliss of the other side.

Elizabeth
August 2008

More

In even still your absence, your silence,
I come to know you more the
Man than I thought to know,
For in your words, your shyful glance and
Smiles, blooms more the sleeping
Baby in innocence's arms.
And what you leave in fair decorum is more
Resplendent abundance over the
Flame of passion's fire, burning out in the
Pain of sensual sweetness.
To receive and comfort me, and touch my soul
With bits of memory's threads,
Yet to look towardward to the complete of
Ivory sentiment which can pour out as
Oil and meal—
I weep, as for a dream, that I held your touch
For a season, to thoughts of more to be,
To lose to more, now, the noblesse of honor
And patience's worth.
My hand catches my throat, my breath
Captured by this thought,
My words faltering in its description,
Save the bleeding of my pen.
There is no love, more, past this
Love of giving, kept.

Elizabeth, in deepest night
August 12, 2008, at the closing, sighing moment
Of the dark rose of midnight—

After visit with R., the first of this year, though
Having had conversations—

157

In early day, I happened by my easel,
And there upon it stood, a canvas, modest,
Repository of left-over paint in various hues—a
Bramble bush, dark, against lighted surface
Behind, but dark, and dark within so that
I could not know its lines.
Out what of me had come this form,
Desperate of joy or light and hope;
I looked inside my conscious self, and there
Again I found the bramble bush,
Silent, intractable, threatening in the impotence it shouted
Out: pouring forth from yesterday, and night
Of present hours housing questions
That answers continue to elude.
The only away is a brush carrying gold, from
A palette provided by generous
Circumstance; the dark will then lighten and begin,
As the dragonfly moving within sunlight,
To take on other colors, forming shape by
Emerging contrast into lines.
And I will quest the gold, out all mysteries and
Happenchance, for inside my awareness, leafed
Of seeds immortal, benevolence
Tendered, the knowing that only acceptance of the
Unknowings, the inconsistencies, the raw meat
Of hard realities—only acceptance of these would
Perfume the spectre they have become,
Keeping out needed light that furnished the gold.
Oh feather of sunflower yellow hue,

Drift lightly over my thought and leave
A rainbow of shadows and bright
That the poor canvas not keep its bramble bush.

Elizabeth, August 14, 2008, having been begun earlier
My parents' birthdays, August 11, 14, in this
Deepest night—

I enjoy these moments of complete aloneness, although
There lies still, on my bed of dreams, an
Emptiness, kept for the treasure of the lines it draws.

The marsh, the bog, yet the heath and the
Bramble, and the darkened grotto—
All, faces of true night,
Unfathomable darkness in the soul.
There is in these only light for the moment,
And it shadowed and failing to
Nothing beyond.
Nor was there any before to which to
Return—only the dark and deep,
And respite in wandering, passing,
Dimming light.

Alone with myself, well I know these
Faces of night; I feel them in my innards
And know their terrible features
With my senses.
Their timbre is tumultuous in my hearing
And of heaviness too great for
Description on my shoulders.
Then, again, as many before: will I stand
Against their strong wind,
Or bend, into its binding clasp.

Elizabeth, August 15, 2008, at twilight
Poor day, mood down, after small rain,
7:30 pm

Wilth Thou go and leave me,
Like time, with gentlest
Farewelling,
Full morning's fairest glory;
Or raven locks, of silkened splendor,
To the swan's midnight's
Polished silver,
Yet the leaf in autumn's radiance
Dying into raw umber's shadow.
Ever is the heart, but its bodice is fickle,
And that inside can but smile,
In some fashion, be alive,
As is its drape, pulled across the moment.
The rainbow arcs not hesitantly,
Nor the bud leave but a faded signature,
The moment forgiving,
And on somewise, with poignant
Forgetting,
Take leave of its rarest, very being.

The great reservoir of spirit is left
But to mourn the forward step.

Elizabeth
August 21, 2008, 9:50 pm
Alone with my thoughts of
The having been—

161

I am found inside the night,
Deepest night,
A soft rain falling, and it is within me,
But as a fire's glow, not cold
Starlight of winter's will,
Yet warm, and, in this moment,
Leaping toward a good passion and a kind
Of peace in its resting.
Small industries and brilliant color
Added to, songs in my heart,
Sweet melodies of yesterday and the
Dance of the morrow—
These redress and strengthen as the
Happy teardrops that anoint my bamboo,
Set outside to enjoy a more nearly heavenly
Refreshment.
I am in the night, I am in the shadow of the
Bamboo, for the day is past, and
It was good, and the night is come,
Finding me, in the moment,
Newly bathed content—
Perhaps moreso because the word "love" was
Sent to me in sweet bonne nuits, quiet unaware,
But so much more in true presence.

Elizabeth, August 24, 2008, about four o'clock am
Mr. Clayton's birthday reminds among my
Steps and innocent willfulness—

I believe, truly, that the chime could sing out
Flowers into the sea of this night, their
Petals as happy hearts, one upon the other,
Weighted by the moment's wetted, joyful peace
Of new awareness.

162

How the single drop widens—
How far into, wanders lifting smoke;
How hard, yet tender the word,
Given voice.
How full with sentiment the all of
Knowing.

Elizabeth
In deepest night, August 27, 2008,
One o'clock pm
Spontaneous fragment—

The late summer afternoon is near to closing
In on me, catching my breath, stilling my heart,
Mourning my thought.
I think of Mamma, sweet olive in oppressive,
Yet declining warmth,
The drone of school buses, and very far
Away, the woodmill at Beauregard;
There are my brownskins, with little
Boy faces, somehow hidden from my sensing touch;
And coming desperately toward me,
Fear of other losses,
Mementoes, order, and comfort.
We lose always, to gather again, but there is
Nothing to, but only remind, be as the first.
Cool evenings are on the palette, as are
Sweetgum leafstars, falling straw in light umber,
And goldenrod; how sweet, the heaviness
To know these, as another
Anniversary that very shouts out presents
Of past days, now put aside, cast into the great
Reservoir of individual recollection.
As surely as the heart remembers, even within
A dusky veil, it bleeds out pure
Crimson,
A flow of loneliness that recalls the pining of
Lovers separated by the cumulative night of
Time, the distance of happenings,
The march of the cell inside its cosem.
Ah, tomorrow calls in September, golden glow
Of aftertime, and my soul yearns

The before and coming after, any to break the
Prison of loss and regret.

Elizabeth, August 31, 2008—

Alone with thoughts, waiting the storm, still again—

Flowers, still in full color wealth,
Dance in geister winds,
And sunlight lingers on the larger
Surfaces, quite forgetting those to the
Aside,
Giving the world of shadow new parameters,
New announcings:
My heart, my heart, let me not know their song,
For I am tender in this moment,
And with their verse would perish of my
Weller self.

September twilight hangs about,
Falling all the full day; the locusts'
Chorus bows to the nightingale, but her
Roses are of dry wine color.

Frangelica after the organ's blue gin on
Summer evening porches; reverie out of
The beautiful dark gold movements when the
Sky is rot—the very feast of life, yet
Its depravity in the larger reality: perhaps
Its quest within our hearts can be a,
Worthy cup, its pathos becoming our own
Crimson to wander with its chest of
Beauty into those of others.
Then, mortal, we—
Insistently, hardly.

Elizabeth, old but familiar stirrings—
Feeling better, of different mood, eventide
This last day of August, 2008

Autumn

I lay in the unsounding dark, companioned
Only by the full heaviness of night
Solitude, its shadows and complete
Absenting.
My life, in dowdy rags, passed all
Before me like a weary dirge,
And I saw, perhaps in first truth, the
Sleight of hand, the covered glance, the quick
Aside, the obligatory stance—
And I knew my aloneness save that I have struggled
Out, built up, out of bramble
Arranged or noted with words which
Were lovely, singularly, out of me, quite
Niggardly of another.
The flower, then, in its complete glory,
To me, does not come except by
My hand, and I know the weight of
Convenience, of circumstance, which on somewise,
I have, in insecurity's press, encouraged,
So that I am, now, empty, my energies used
Up; and to this moment adds the
Conclusion of knowing nothingness,
My heart pale, my soul washed through,
That as unacknowledged, and taken as the
Ever useful prop: thankless gratitude,
Unengaged company, that near at hand,
Forgetting all.

Elizabeth, September 5, 2008, nine-thirty pm
Hours alone of those of any true care—

What the night does not show is as the basket
Empty, yet offered up.

169

September Eve

Oh Thou, All Good that is,
Fill me in my poverty as surely Thou had'st
In my fullness, for the sun has been
Long in its journey to me, and I
Have been this day, most, grey
Smoke desperately lifting, but with emptiness,
To find the vaulted, joyful blue.
Now that shadows are pushed, briefly,
Aside, I know Ariel steps again,
In truth, of Thy willing, the sun
Only watchful.
Help me to know larger portions of the
Circle as my path continues,
And allow these wisdoms to comfort and strengthen
Even into recollection,
Alive, with laughter and song.

Elizabeth, about four o'clock Saturday,
September 6, 2008

A long, grey, and until now, difficult day of spirit—
Gold and silver press for catching, but
As I, in yearning, true, reach—
Peace, please, peace: safety from fear
And lodging in care, Thy tenuous, porcelain
Doll, again, in tender hands.

170

September's Time

September time, that of resting, laying by,
    Companioned by memory paths,
Revisited, dreams, from distances,
        Recounted.
There is not the beautiful fury of scarlet,
    Flamed fire, but the loveliness,
The better warmth left over of glow,
Yet golden, gentler, forgiving and leaning
        Into peace.
Bittersweet, as the fragrant Sweet Olive,
    Darker hues with silver begin to
Appear and the adventures they foretell.
How much in the heart lies the pulsating,
    If impotent ember, to somehow,
Out desperation's last, rise and bloom
In finality, its most splendid flower—
A second summer, its imaged presence,
To continue into the forever it portends.
Sweet, sweet, this house of sentiment,
    This giving, this taking,
    This making of peace—
        This September.

Elizabeth, Sunday morning, about 10:00
        September 14, 2008

All thoughts unbrellaed—

My way passed through low lying clouds
With the infant sun laughing into the lesser
Gold of my citrine;
Trees arranged as draped appointments,
Nature's rooms comfortable in
Their patterns and dusky, smoke-like
Breath,
All among what was to be September greens.
Goldenrod strewn all about, not yet
Donning its clarion hue, and crepe myrtle
Began to step into place,
The southern lady in her softness and grace.
Dew happily anointed florets and buds
Before the accomplishment of later hours.
Such pastoral scenes wove beautylove into my
Senses, and with thoughts of men
And industry setting in place,
Dissonance rang into the placid quiet.
Faraway I must keep these frames, their gift
Of joy inside their loveliness,
Almost holy in a journey bound with a
Reality which aches the senses
And fills the heart with Roman murmurings.

Elizabeth, on driving to class—
September 17, 2008,
About seven o'clock am

172

I am, with a hesitant, but groomed patience,
Coming to find a pleasing contentment
In my loneliness—
Like settling down among
Deep covers,
Finally to discover, to feel
The comfort of warmth from cold.
Being in company, listening, conversing,
And touching
Fill a portion of my need, but
It is as though I am on a train, it moving
Quickly, quickly,
And I cannot sit, wishing, almost
With a prayer, to stop and board off.
I want to share with others, yet keep all truly
For myself, the inner experiencing of every sentiment,
Just to know as my own, to,
Speaking Rilke, "build myself a [winter]," a season.
Surely, then, I could remember, and know,
Experience and feel, quite without
The varied dissonances that are constant to me.
Ah soul, Beggar in nobility,
Let me know, let me feel that that I am,
Clothed in solitude, hued of nothing,
Yet in fancy and in my raw flesh,
Know the beauty of my full
Humanity.

The closet will not wear, alone, and close,
Nor the fair with its gatherings,
And open; somewhere, sometime,
There must come a ceremony.
A consented marriage.

Elizabeth, September 19-20, 2007

The Lighted Knowing

Found in these late hours of
Earliest morning,
When quiet hangs over the moving
Color of night as surely as
Its darkened hue,
I heard once, and then a second time,
The plaintive cry of a distant owl,
Faint as in a farewelling,
It falling into, and enlarging my
Knowing solitude.
Thee and me, owl, perhaps with souls
More kindred than can ever be
Declared;
But ah, I know of it, and it is unto
Thee
As Thy feathers, Thy visage, only
Real to the darkness of which Thou art,
Leaving me alone, in pain of the
Light of knowing.

Elizabeth, in deepest night,
September 21, 2008, about 3:30 am

As the recognizable sting of the unseen dart,
In its first purposed freedom,
My thought reached to companion
The images offered,
They within early morning dust-grey,
And stillness that dressed the room's
Life in its newest promise.
Like a cat that moves in cautious,
Deftly shadowed steps,
Like a cinema's still,
Without announcement, that awakens,
The light, in anemic strength,
Poured life onto the straight-back chair, the
Flowing silk roses, the mirrors
Filled with their instant catchings.
Surreal feelings cuckolded me, made me drunk
With half belief, and I entered the
World of the concrete real,
Hesitatingly, unwantingly, the
Wandering through of the abstract true
Whom those others saw and knew, in what they
Thought my unknowing, they,
The wise lessors.

Elizabeth, in deepest night,
October 2, 2008—
About 2:30 am

An image courting my thought as I passed
Into sleep, anticipating the
New day—

175

The early October cool lightly
Moved over my rooms, over my person,
But, most, over my heart,
In its pensive aching, petals of summer's
Loveliness blown away with its
Flowing soul.
My heart accepted the gentle sensation,
Quietly, mournfully, out poverties
Waiting as light in a partially opened door—
To stream out and over into full knowing
Under the hurt that called insistently,
With harsh press to my fullest
Understanding.
Like fruit on a table to be arranged for
Painting, players, events, and, more, feeling—
These arrange here and there, but
The canvas concludes with color and
Form that are always the same
In the afterglow;
The perspective is just moved a portion
There or there.
Lovely, young, and raven, matroned,
Years accomplished into silver, my heart is
With itself, none to touch, none to say,
While the progression of time continues into
Conclusion.
What heaviness, what grief that as much seen
To be offered and given now moves
Lightly over my heart, my thought, and
Finally into the lost away.

Elizabeth, October 4, 2008, about 10:30 pm
Alone—

When full night is come in every face
With peace, the beauty of forgiving is chanson
To all, and petals fall in syncopated lyrics,
Counterpointed appointments, sentiments
Of finest, silkened threads of
Melodies woven over the sands kind winds
Bring out and about to sing and flow,
These about their fertile gardens of
Innocence and knowing.
Oh, Night, visage of ease,
Fragranced of yesterday and dreams of coming
Wonderment, stay this while, and let it
Be ebonied solitude of sweetest, dark-honeyed mead;
And let the comfort of that unseen remain
In heart stalwart and brave, but they, yet,
Enjoy and take Thy ease close to repose,
So that when the faintest light in grey climbs
Onto the canvas of being, there will be the
Peace, the ease, the repose of something
Kept of the veil of white, flowing
In lovely rounds for all who look to see.

Elizabeth, October 5, 2008,
About 10:30 pm
From a sense of tranquil thought and
Unstimulated, non-purposeful movement—

The pale gold butterfly, after moving with grace in patterns
So that the sun can only know—
Quiet now, with gentlest breath—

In ode-like proclamation, I have declared
That never more would
Bear a cleavage, be brought more the
Weight of heaviness in loss,
The complete ambiance of grey
In hope—
These, and in greater passion, never more come
To me again.
I thought my heart in its former tender
Of pain would not be met again
In superlative stance, that my
Magnanimous given care was all that
There was, and in my cordial
Munificence had gifted in feeling, all.

And now, in these late, earliest morning hours,
A melody of time past has brought again the loss,
The reality of the loss,
Its irretrievable capture—
And I knew it was then the fullest, the complete,
The undying remnant,
And it was, is, again—felt the more.

Elizabeth, October 5, 2008, about 10:30 am—
In my bedroom midst the absolute glory of
The beauty of October
In Mississippi

Thinking back to early morning hours, weary
In patience for day and falling prey to
Music which made my heart to bleed,
Yes, the more, taunted, again—

178

In the become friendly stranger
Of night, I moved through simple, timeless
Industries, and my gaze fell upon
Red variegated rose petals,
Dried and gathered into a painted
Espresso cup, long ago brought from the
Continent.
Within the dust being removed, I saw
Great beauty; the light on the balcony was
Alive, but motionless, and the clock
Sounded continually passing moments into
Eternity while lavender, from its pillow,
Rested its shadow throughout
The breath of the rooms.
Good and evil, together, never were;
Beauty in its world of constancy was all.
Woundings were lifted away
By lighted streams falling over,
Rouge and ivory, restoring into wholeness
Distant paths.
The wonderment of time and its
Accompaniments fell a peace inside the
Petals, into my aloneness,
From within this friendly stranger
Bringing, innocently,
Gifts warm and generous, but resting
Against the realities of
New day.

Elizabeth
In deepest night, about 3:30 am,
July 18, 2008

Two fragments found recently, and put together—
The meaning is unclear now—
October 5, 2008, 4:00 am

And in my heavy fatigue, my growing wanting need,
I dreamed of springtime faery trees and pebbles,
Very tulips of Old Provence; and peacock
Feathered waters flowing down the
Soft lay of the colors.
The time was quiet, and soft, respite for
Longest effort and wait, for tears kept
In desperate prisons, growing larger
Than darkened gardens.
Music visited my ear, and it was sweet,
Like hymns among summer dahlias
Gathered with sprinklings of light from
Gentle insects that bless with their cheer.
Let me so sleep, let me so not think but dream
The dahlia hymns, the flowing waters—
The beauty in trees that burst out
In movement's wonderment.
Banish, oh self of mine, those words and
Scenes that bring pain of beauty lost,
Yet into today's hours of emptiness
And lonely vigil that has become
The silent butler, that into which I sweep my acceptance,
To place temporarily aside—
A courtesy, as it were,
When I wake.

Elizabeth, October 7, 2008
About 7:00 pm

181

I am weary with inconsistencies, inconstancies,
Infidelities, and unadulterated falsehood,
Yet humor out of anger and sayings
That move toward conversation untrue,
Courtesies ingenuinely extended.
The clock nor the calendar are honored,
Or, more, the word, spoken, it
Though with greatest authority and feigned
Verity.
Waiting is difficult, as is deciphering the
Error that is thought to be overlooked,
Or else, I be shouted out the rigid, the ungiving,
The anchorite, musing malevolence.
Where is the straight path, the lane that
Protected the promenade of gentlemen and ladies.
And the docile kine.
Was there ever the pure pastoral when promise
Of certainty was celebrated, a press now
That the dew sparkled, that noonday was
Brightest, ever, and sunset pleasant,
Closing repose.
Can there be no more certainty, press that
Drives to distraction, confusion of truth, in self
And others, ultimately pushing toward alienation
And the absolute of the garden where one
Is at peace, only alone.

Elizabeth, October 9, 2008, about 6:30 pm

Nothing is as it purports to be,
Or else the climes and the seasons
Of my thought are leaning toward confusion.

182

Petaled flown winds from summer's
Hesitating sighs,
Sunlight, small lad slightly moving, yet
So into the waiting, resting, unrequiring
Distance;
The grace of the moving of beautifully
Masculine bamboo portal centers,
Allowing natural stances that catch
The heart;
And lying in modest, alert repose, the morning's
Gift of wetted diamonds, in the benevolence of
October beginning light:
How could not there be all good, if losing
Its path at certainty's behest,
But in the round, where we are all eventually
Found—
In the balance—
Good, all good.

Elizabeth, October 11, 2008, about 5:30 pm
Twilight's approach to the close of a
Beautiful autumn day—

Even dimly hued shadows appear colorings pouring
Down over familiar friends, suggesting
A gentleness in All Kind as we enter the long
Path of night, it strewn with darkly crimsoned
Roses to pleasure nightingales, their fragrance
Laying a pallet for wandering spirits
To lightly touch the earth—
In the balance, good, all good—

183

I sense that I am near to the turn, for I
Cannot more bear the intensity
Of my thought, my many passions.
I am alienated from all, the voiceless
Wind wandering the earth, the tedium of
Sameness and confusion; I am as deeply
Dark as is the night, and I am left spent
At day's end with the pulsating
Of the hours of lighted brilliance—
More, none know of these tryings,
These fullnesses, their left emptinesses—
Or, with reason's humbleness—
That I know, more than exception in
Glimpses there and here that promise and
Flourish—
Ah, the joy in these rare moments,
But to come, their certain metamorphosing,
To become unpatterned, to dim and wander away
Into the empty promise of their nativity.
Oh soul, Thou of my knowing, give me
Content in part, or else give me
Wholeness in part. I cannot anymore,
Or so now it seems, that I can see, to feel—
Beauty beyond the power of words to draw, and
It always as the grail, elusive, evading,
Being held out in the fore, to promise and
Tease, and to then lift as a sigh into
An enchanted emptiness.

I think, at times, that I am too strong to turn
The turn, but, oh, too tender to stand
In the indecision of leaning.

Elizabeth, October 14, 2008

184

Oh Thee of my inner most, my sensing, feeling of
Wanting, needing, sighs of absence and
Emptiness—
Where the laughter found and lifted away,
Touch as passionate fire burning,
Washed burnt, away—
Now thoughts run into the edges, words
Falling to the aside, but all away—

The riddle of beauty to become a nothing
In reality, or perhaps always was in its true being—
But in the crimson inner most, real, sweet,
And tender, and in these lost,
All lost other than now in the bittersweet
Of scenes romanced by senses, lonely, hungry,
Wishing to give that they receive—
Something to carry away to the pillow, the arm,
The cheek resting on linens which
Are real in the morning carrying glimpses of what
Was, has been, if only a partial apparition,
Beautiful in its wistfulness,
It portioned real and fancied.

Thoughts to go to bed on—
Elizabeth, October 16, 2008
About 10:00 pm
Some confusion with what is real—

Words, smiles, petals falling into flowing water,
Summertime over all—how could this be but love,
If but for a season—
Love, love—energy that lives into the ever, no matter
The form, guise, fashion: the electric impulse continues—

Gentle, birthing rain, now in forgotten
Hours, those dark that will not be more,
I hear, out silence as flow, rain in contented falling,
Like glimpses in yesterday, whispers, sighs
And tears, as if there is no trumpet to sound,
And soon, to know the flowering,
The moving breath of day.
Content are the legions of October raindrops,
With unbroken cadence, as if they will
Always be, the comfortable, possessed now;
But comes again the trumpet, though in dress
Of grey—
Still it will come and all will have no sense
Of the content, only night passed
Into day.

A brief realization of the power of the
Natural, of one ambiance nature can wield
To the open, listening spirit—

Elizabeth, in deepest night,
October 17, 2008, about 3:15 am

Oh, what charity to soul would be,
While on my arm I sleep, in sleep of every
Unknowing,
That happiness would, in some distant
Province, billow up in all beauty and good,
To come and spread over me, a
Coverlet of peace and quiet glory—
One in Scheherazade lights of
Pleasing hues, in form both numerous and
Fair, haloed by sighs of benevolent
Offerings.

So difficult are some hours that the antidote
Of beauty can usher in through
Medicinal, visiting happiness,
And the joy of being turns round again from
Darkened, shadowed climes; then can Helen
Poise, again, to launch, Isadora, again,
Flower, to dance, and as far as
Winding, fabled threads may wander,
Cinderella may once more step into her
Faery-touched glass slipper.

Elizabeth, October 21, 2008
12:45 am

After day of desperate thoughts and turnings toward
An uneasy peace—

The time is falling twilight,
The light taking its leave hesitatingly,
Drawing behind its shadows,
Passively moving, defeated chariots,
October aware now of still another
Season of repose.
The silence is very close to full knowing,
The millions of small bells
Ringing together, just beside unison,
Unveiling the nothingness
Hanging all about.
Images visit, in and out, like beautiful
Turning serpents, their heads
Increasing in numbers as they pierce
The coming dark, their emeraled and
Rubied eyes suggestive floral
Stings.
I do not wish anything, I think, in this
Moment, for I am too weary
To know need or desire, only
To conclude without a careful heaviness
Of questions, or any overfull cup of
Bittersweet.

Elizabeth, October 25, 2008
At twilight
Of a long, difficult day of mood
Remaining down—

Ah, sweet creature, winged of gold,
Fly quickly now into my rooms,
My mood, for the night has passed long,
On the other side of ever,
And I wish to see the splendor of
Wetted stones as they slowly enter
From their pretending,
They on the chilled hues of early autumn
Leaves—those which verily shout out the
Voice of beauty in the clarity of
October bright.
I am enamored by the gentle movement of the
Waiting, quiet stillness, the joyful
Songs of woodland choruses, and feel
The rapture of brilliance in beauty
Innocence among the natural and free.
Let me know, always, and hold, before I forget
In dayful musings, that my heart not have the
Poverty of less than the full gift of
Creation.

Elizabeth, October 26, 2008
At sunrise, until about nine o'clock;
So heavy with sleep, losing portions of
The impressions:
Cycled up again during the night—

Looking back on the beauty of the pain
In the gold before the more gold—
If only I could know them within tense—

189

And so the days were filled up with
Their doings, and the years
Accumulated their collections
So that sentiment was felt and put aside
As garments worn and ready to
Be cast into the dark, until the next
Time.
Somehow, in this ritual of natural behaviors,
Time takes the individual, the unique,
The select and rare—
The celebrated—
And all is lulled into a half-dream that
Was a time of being and feeling,
But its purpose was to be stepped away,
To be caught, perhaps, in some
Lovely narrative that pulsates in its
Recitation—
But most, into forgetfulness, without
Angst, guilt, or remorse, but a
Gentle fatigue of acceptance—
In the stepping lay a mystic, uncommon
Glory, a fullest recompense,
Veiled and rent.

Elizabeth, October 30, 2008
About midnight
The close of a lovely October day,
Reflection brought to my thought by an insistent
Muse: pardon—

When the sunlight fails to fall lightly,
Faintly, on the cool October leaves,
In these, its final hours,
I will draw the door and
The season of cold will be with us—
We each, as in all seasons,
Microcosms of this experience we call
Being, existence, in which we
Live and in which
We die,
Within, and among our
Importances.

Elizabeth, October 31, 2008
At twilight, 5:45 pm

After just having read and lectured on
G. Flaubert's short story
"A Simple Heart"—

My gaze, of no will or plan, falls on the
Bouquet of white with yellow
Chrysanthemums and those together
Of purist white,
Appointed into fuller beauty by
Scarlet begonias.
They stand tall and with lovely grace while
Nature is requiring the blood of
The begonia into an ashened, dry flesh.
When the stubbles move quickly, harshly, and
With piercing stings,
And the falls control with cruel, harsh blows,
Bludgeoning almost unable to bear,
It is difficult to say that all will be well;
But some, many stand in lovely grace, just
At the moment that the last drop of wet is lifted
From its flesh—
All around and intermingled stand the lovely graced
And our jaundiced eye can only see that
Falling.
Perhaps the greatest wisdom we can know is
Of the lovely grace, the greatest curse
Awareness that fallings come,
Attended by the loneliness of this knowing
Without camaraderie in its fullest
Coming, as a drape, as a pall complete,
Without interruption to finality,
This promise visited upon us.
Elizabeth, November 2, 2008
About 9:40 am

Ebonied Panther, One

September sunlight has held its melancholy
Across her beginning gold, through
October's clarity, and into November's
Coming benediction.
Falling summer's windsongs have
Stayed their while, late, late, so that it is
With a sigh that they kiss our cheek
In anticipation fatigued of sentiment begun
With first whispers.
The moon is distantly chilled, now, rather
Than demurely serene,
And cannot gather more left-over
Beauty of prosperous sunlight. The moonflower,
Marvelous in its loveliness, is a cold
Memory, and the coming day's sun cannot
Bring back its passion, not until
Another walk through dark and memory,
Waiting the new.
Oh, melancholy, darkened rose of sweetest
Ambiance, sentiment of present youth
And fullest reflection, why does't thou court all
That is beautiful to finally, purposefully
Wander about it, declaring its passing.

Open the belly of the ebonied panther
And let the gold inside spill out over, for some,
Without its intense power, will remain

In the familiar ritual,
But the seed, unable to reach, to lie
In dark and dust.

Elizabeth, November 6, 2008, 6:15 pm
After receiving class year book
A German reference

Ebonied Panther, Two

I hear, within the deep of my pleasant solitude,
The sounds of movement of all things,
And I know that it is day;
I see the gold of November, inside small rain,
Throughout the whole of my thought,
And I know gratitude.
Oh God of my heart, undrawn by my reason,
But true in my being,
Save this glory for me, that I be
Imbued with the beautywealth of a
Noblewoman, to hold now, presently,
And recapture when it is yesterday—
For I sense flowers of good, also,
In these moments sweet, come to visit me,
Clasping my hands,
Holding them fast.

The gold of the ebonied panther flowed out
In the night, and has washed me with
The powerful strength of his treasure
So that I reach and grow,
Think and feel;
Dust, today, is but an unfortunate construct.

Elizabeth,
Resting after lunch on November 7, 2008

Very good class today—haiku—
About 12:55 pm
A German reference

Whether through a round of brilliantly
Lighted gold,
Or
Flowing out to all that is fed by is
River of strength,
God is, present and within,
Glory manifest in beauty, the greatest
Truth beside ultimate truth.
How but to rejoice, to be glad—and
In the shadowed recess of memory, the
Boon of yesterday, an operatic
Line out my voice of prophetic holding:
"Look, the sun, the sun...."
Speaking then into now with growing
Strength, it sounds before, now, ever.

Elizabeth, November 9, 2008
About nine-forty five am

A beautiful sunrise, as if surely the only, the first
To Autumn's glory—

Mood enhanced and courage offered—

I know it is less and less simply because
There is less of it.
The hours take bits and pieces, the days
Whole portions, and new paths
Call to wander, indeed, insist to step,
Leaving old walks to backward
Advancing.
The roses, the violets, winds that dance
With light and shadow as
Small butterflies in their summer frolic—
Sprites, they all, touching for a moment's
Pleasure:
And when a constancy we hold closely
Familiar, newly arriving seasons—
When these come, at first, in kindness of
Color and breath—
We are gifted, for the moments of them
We daily lose, and the roses are there, as
The creekside violets, the gentle winds that
Blow peace into our places.
These jewels, beautiful stones in a
Magnificent tapestry, shine brightly in their
Time, and hold in store that that we
Lose, more and more, to want our gathering,
All in newness, fully detailed of glorious
Lines—
All when we step through, for that is the only
Way that we can conceive for our poor kind.

Elizabeth, November 11, 2008
1:40 pm

Confused thoughts—

197

I find, in present days, my foot upon the
Floral stepstool that it is pleasurable
To look forward to a small nap.
And even more
Pleasure finds in anticipating
The feeling of promised renewal,
Of beginning again, small mornings, as it were,
Inside the day, after the nap is
Finished.
But in the immediate afterwards, the
Pleasure lifts away, become caught into the
Routine of a day of tired sameness
And innocent idleness.
I know that I am wandering away from
Something, somewhere very close to me,
Beautiful, full, with grief to the side,
Toward something, somewhere I cannot
Yet construct into idea or conceive
In sentiment.
Ought is that I know certainly that my
Nap pleasure, in the balance,
Conversely darkens me, making me
Full of a heavy song of sorrow.

Elizabeth, November 11, 2008
About 2:30 pm

Upon rising from a well thought nap,
But—
Thoughts, thoughts—

Finding early morning, darkness offered a wide
Pillow on which I lay, in the softness,
Content.
And music moved over me in beautiful hues
Of voice that touched the innermost
Part of my needing, wanting self;
I remembered the lingering, smaller
Rounds of departing sunlight in yesterday's
Afternoon.
They were as bright as morning's bright,
Moving there and about, giving their
Same gold.
Oh, Time, in early morning's dark,
And under the romance of music, the sweet
Memory of gold stepped away, give to me,
Today, the left-over gold again, that
The arms of beauty my soul sits vigil to,
Come again, with caresses tender and
Filling, complete.

And the crimson floral, velveted coverlet
Let fall its tassels with my tears of recognition—
As long as it is, the flower of joy can open,
More than in loveliness of the
Widow's mite, willingly taken in the
Full opulence of matroned gratitude.

Elizabeth, November 18, 2008

Under new age music in gentle light of small dark,
Content in the moment, its beauty
And wisdom—
About three o'clock am

199

There is not anything into the away, becoming
The far away, as poignant as forgotten loss;
Memory and sentiment continue, but accompanied,
Most, by emptiness of the pathos of first
Grief when all of the small and large
Importances weep their, now,
Lacking.
The egalitarian prince of time wields,
With strength, his two-edged sword:
Content in distant sorrow that no longer
Touches but images out respectful pensiveness
Whose echoes, whose haloes, whose
Whispers cannot be but of greyest
Hue.

In theory, and classes thereof, this
Phenomenon is labeled
Neatly,
Tied into a welcomed package, often
Quite attractive, called
"Adjustment."

What we lose we do keep, in a hidden
Silence,
And it can be found in the wistful
Sigh.

Elizabeth, early morning, five o'clock
November 20, 2008

We write of the universe
Of ourselves,
As all that inside a raindrop,
Mirrored a microcosm
Of the macrocosm of
Existence,
Of Humankind.

Elizabeth, November 22, 2008

After classes, studying three twentieth
Century major poets, of India,
China, and Russia—
World Masterpieces course—
Mississippi College,
Clinton, Mississippi

The sun is entering my gentle rooms
Like a huge day star, pulsating brightest
Light that can have color, and
I am joyful that I am well-minded
In good weather.
Hope is present as a vast umbrella,
Spreaded, that will not close, not until
The like of a day finishing in summer,
Long down a dusty, friendly
Road which winds as far as memory
Generously calls.
Good comes at these such times, for there
Is all about the ambiance of good,
Pouring forth, streaming down,
The very complexion of good, with
Falling movements, laughing charms,
On this day unfolding, full.
New blue, small feathers, rich, gold on
Pumpkins' rounds, dream-like glistening
Of frozen dew on quieted grasses—
And dancing leaves—
These good, abundant good in early
Morning moments.

Elizabeth, November 25, 2008
About eight o'clock am

I awakened, suddenly, full audience to
Thundering silence, such that I
Engaged all thought
To a reprieve.
And I found the dozen white roses,
Sisters to my thousand white gardenias,
And their purity of gifting by the lone
Raven, man-child.
Together, these juxtaposed with the
Complete finality of the dead, the great
Distance of the forgetting, the emptiness
Of the feigning.
And the composite did bend me, the
Innocent love that danced lightly in new candle
Light, a dozen, flawless white roses,
Inside the disfiguring heaviness of the silence
Of all other that fell around me.
I am alone in winter, alone save my roses
That could not, even with their smiles of care,
Shadow the reality of their singularness;
And this knowing, in recurring, pulsating,
Wave-like silence, pressed my spirit,
Leaving my soul in company of
The castaway.

Elizabeth, November 30, 2008
Four o'clock am, having passed through still
Another reminder—
A very grande, personal malaise courts my
Whole self;
Now is the coldest portion of the day—

Winter

205

I have placed you in a tower, one that
The silver falcon does not touch in its
Circlings,
This tower of rose marble that keeps
Inside your smile, your laughter
At good wit, your remembered
Touch, stolen but of
Passionate warmth.
You are there in distance from me,
Clouds and mists closeting any image,
The physical distance, high into its spires
Removing your person;
But the heart is a living fountain
That flows as long as there is
Cognizance of its sentiment.
You, away in your tower, left below
My second gardenias, the sunshine,
The completeness which enlarges in its
Lack of consummation.
Tower, tower, undefined distance—
I know your rooms hold that that the
Chambers of my heart only in rarest moments,
Embraces.

Elizabeth,
December 1, 2008
9:45 pm

Thoughts, long, long thoughts—

The three o'clock hour, every night,
Is the coldest,
Its silence most present,
The lamp appearing in familiar fatigue,
The chime moving almost without motion.
Three is an ancient symbol, a number
Reminding completion:
The sun, at its point of greatest distance,
Is there only to turn, back to us, bringing the
Warmth we cherish and use as
A relic to kiss in adoration, over which to
Offer prayers, that the three o'clock
Be only one hour of chill,
A strikingly clever metaphor of the true
Death of the day, giving rise to a
Virgin day, full of purist light and the
Beautiful carnival of living and being.

Elizabeth, December 2, 2008
3:15 am

A phenomenon I have come to observe
In these nocturnal moments of
Pensiveness—

A Christmas Fantasia

Oh, little images, queenly portions of spirit,
Cast not anymore looks of dismissal
Toward me, I, lady to Thy
Hearth and fire.
On parting and arriving, no words fall
Into the silence, of either farewell
Or greeting so that I stand as one of stone,
Yet bound dust in death, unacknowledged,
And I pass Thee off as the moments
Of an idle hour.

But the real does not, indeed, govern, yet
With the sceptre held out, for though
It is difficult for children, we dance in light
As nymphs and fairies, sprites and
Sylphs, feeling and sensing wearing
Crown to reason, our fountainhead,
The harp, the lyre through which
Flows our steps and fullest being.

Ought else, but to give over to the
Christmas in us, the innocent, giving and
Tender of rarest truth: that our
Formulae call for precision and contact,
But better to let away birds and butterflies
Into the vast openness, petals pulled and strewn
Into the outward, and to add a rush of cadmium light,
A splash of thalo green, and give to the
Wind to kiss us with first beauty.

Good, God Almighty, life is a feast,
A fire raging as flame of scarlet leaping
With all the force of its passion,
Into it most intense of purist white:
Andso, all that is, can be, come!

To the inward eye, in the open meadow,
Time and space dance a minuet
In us all, and we, with partners fair, marry
The sensual and spirit-laden, following the
Rich threads of wandering tapestry hues,
The sensation of wealth in velvet texture,
And the risk of touch to icy satin.
Let, more, our hearts to know the
Tryst with passion, just beside reason, the
Full glory of our sensual selves that is galley
To spirit and impetus to sports of
Reason.

Birds, now, as close to spirit as are
Thy hearts, let not to lose a recognition of a reality
I cannot bear, for I am sensation
And thought, forced to step by pattern's
Authority, but oh, with Beethoven's
Heaviness and the pubescent lightness
Of his fellow—

I wing with these into the gold of the day's
Awareness where colors laugh and
Sounds touch—
And—

209

I lie in fullness of beautiful and wounding
Longings, the rainbow, the peacock,
The frolic of sunlit dew, with my lovers
Who dream me into an intensity
Which escapes Thy flight, all inside
Silent whispers of lovely images,
Sonnets to soul, and wealthy chest to
Ecstasy that walks past standing
Commands.

Berries and florets, pears and the ancient
Gourd, the crimson wet of
Cherryripe, and the blue of sky, alone of
Other, spread out before me with the
Delicate of figmeat beside the ivory
Purity of breasts wounded in the press of
Sentiment—
These all fill hourly my senses that the
Birds be cuckolded in their
Improprieties to my whole self, my spiritual
Musings which court fantasy and pleasure,
Silent tribute to that of me that closets
The fire of the gold inside the
Panthered form of "good mind" and of
Circumstance, bound to wear.

Andso at Christmas lies the rarest rose.

Elizabeth, in deepest night,
December 7, 2008, 3:15 am

The coldest hour—
A reply to the birds, the raging of my silent thought—

So heavy the weeping into the
Greater urn of allness—

Blowing wheat and lifting lavender,
Into summer morning's lighted
Counterpoint: these touched by the
Lying down of winter's rose and purple
In sunsets, lying down these holding in
Leaf patterns shadowing the
Sweet pungence of the faithful, waiting
Flesh of earth.

Good, God Almighty, grant to us all the
Feast already given as only Christmas
Can remind.

Elizabeth afterthought

And the birds do not ever see my glow—
Most sad comment to my soul—
At Christmas—

The morning came in, somehow, light
Finding lines and masses turning
Into shaped forms,
And there also arrived sound,
Not to me, but around me.
And I knew that life breathed, again,
Into the departing darkness.
These, all, were like expected visitors,
And brought respite to the pall
Of emptiness that covers me,
But they quickly evolve into mirrors
That chide, for their wares reflected do not
Emit from me or any of mine,
But the open expanse of the wideness that
Does not see or hear me, knowing
Only that I am a being without
Qualities: no needs, no grace,
No generosities to offer.

I am buttressed by my solitude, and it offers me
The sustenance to stand and view, to know,
But not to touch.
Within my self is my only self, and as the desert fathers,
I live and breathe within, and die inside the
Expanse of every moment.

Elizabeth, December 18, 2008
About eleven am

The Yellow Christmas Daisy

Still another of those especially intense, but
Curiously lovely moments is visiting
Me again.
In these impatient hours just before light,
When darkness still paints out all
Detail, I can see the one, lone yellow
Daisy I discovered yesterday, closeted
Within wet ivies and brown, cold winter straw.
It was magnificent, a circle surely of a pale
Yellow painted dish, its petals lying
In perfect form, joining to a jewel-like center.
And I wish, now, to go out to it, to gather
Its beauty unto me, even in darkness where
There is no light to see; I am under great
Press to go out to the blossom.
These whispered, almost mystical moments
Come to me now and again, often
When I need my saving antidote to despair,
More when it seems impossible to claim
Them.
But beauty, in reality or fancy, is good, and
Serves well my soul, perhaps with greatest care
When it is near, but beyond my reach,
Stretching, then, my senses to receive it.
Oh night, fly thee to thy resting chamber,
And leave me in presence of the yellow

Christmas daisy, perhaps, heretofore, in
Unseen glory, giving out of season.

Elizabeth, December 19, 2008, 5:45 am
Dr. Norton has spoken to me of taking care
In these such moments.

The day is, with purposed steps,
Moving into twilight and still,
Silence becoming across the light
Now covered most by spreaded raven wings.
Oh sting of the moment passed,
Yesterday is pressing in on the present
Real of feeling and thought:
Will they die into the infinite or be caught
In part with words and song—
Or, perhaps, in haloes, whispers, sighs
That are spontaneous liftings from the fire,
The energy of this path now laid out,
To wander into tomorrow with its
Joy and sorrow.

Then and now—
Ever and always—
Words and constructs yielding the
Messages of life: but oh, in feeling, aware,
And, more, richly veiled,
Swelling up and passing—this was the all
Of it; and nowhere—in the tears of twilight,
The pain of darkness, the absent touch of still—
Can it, again, be found.

Elizabeth
December 21, 2008

At twilight, in hard cold

Oh Mien Dieu, there is a silence in the dark,
And dark in this new day,
Beginning
Christmas Day:
In the still of the flower opening out
The dark and quiet,
Is memory the sweetness we hold to,
Is now the unfortunate real we
Stand apart from,
And hope,
As the flower unfolds into joyous light
And day,
The opening of a newness, a good of
Old wine with new spirits, hope
Leading doubt into peace, peace that
Charms even now, falling about this first
Moment of backward glance,
And recognition.

Questions, against time, fall gracefully
To answers.

Elizabeth, December 25, 2008
About 6:30 am

A very peaceful, satisfying eve into day—
Birdcalls and soft rain, intermittently—

This Season

In the new life that is morning,
Small industries, to the shadowed
Side of those greater,
Offer up testament to the full of hope
And joy:
The new candle flame leaping with its
First glowing;
Water in its advent flow, clear and fresh,
New to Christian hands;
The golden leviathan rising, finally, into
His whole being, out the jeweled blue
Whale-road of his night;
And the tender shoot, yet in winter, pushing
With humble might, knowing to us,
The earth moving.
Great is the benevolence of force and
Energy that place us in these
Awarenesses and sweet the fragrance
Of their being.

Elizabeth, December 28, 2008
About 10:30 am

Thoughts—good thoughts, dressed with humility—

And in this continuing, gentle reverie, the
Image of the holly berry presses my
Inward eye, its varying, wetted hues of rouge

217

As Sabbath matins' rays play about its cheeks:
How truly beautiful this season of scarlet gems
Upon a fair linen of nature's
Velvet green—

I embrace it all, and throw it,
In its entire, back into the away;
That is the only true pattern,
As the turns and twines of a lace motif—
No beginning or ending, only
Movement within, without into the given
Wide expanse, to the seam which
Contains the flow.

Ought is to hope that the movement is
Kind to give many worlds in many
Moments before our knowing quietens them—
And then that the knowing is
Generous in the reprieve of a long
Forgetfulness.

I acknowledge the loss in self defense—
For to struggle against the reality
Of no prize is folly into madness.
And acceptance is not a prize:
It is an only given condition that
We can know.

Elizabeth
December 30, 2008
About four o'clock am

A concluding thought, over again—

Dedicatory Twilight
My Firelighter
Absent Laughter
The Color of Rose

My Firelighter

Brightly colored threads
Wind their way through a tapestry of love;
Some are the showing of golden rod and morning-glories,
Or being invited to eat
A ripe fig, fresh from the tree;
But now, as summer gives into fall,
I see one thread that shines more brightly.
A little girl who saw dragons
And other creatures in the dark of moonless winter nights,
I looked longingly at the one,
Roughed in window of the cold bedroom
Where I slept with my three brothers.
All I needed was a little light to chase away the monsters.
But it was bedtime
And oil for the lamp was dear;
Enough wood for fires was difficult to find and gather.
And then Mamma would open the door to her room,
Which was also the fireplace room;
Somehow she would find enough pieces
To build again a small fire from the glowing coals.
When the fire was burned,
I was asleep,
Saved again,
By my gentle firelighter.

1990's

Absent Laughter

I sat in early morning,
And I listened to the world awaken to day,
My corners and windows
Throwing off the cover of darkness.
An old account comes to mind of a chore
My mother discharged in these hours each day
For her stepfather.
She was, always, to rise early
And go the barn and lot,
To separate the cows and calves
For feeding and milking.
Not in her tenth year,
She was tender and innocent,
Like a pure white flower in an oppressive darkness.
By this and other circumstances,
She was gravely wounded;
Somehow, perhaps of desperate prayer
And attentive angels,
She pulled out of her soul
Great strength and good,
But I never heard my mother laugh.

Undated, late 1990's

Of my mother, the early
Darkness visited to her,
And then to me;
No one knows this circumstance,

223

For it was recounted to me
Alone, her child—
Mother who listened and
Comforted out resources
Used, and later used
Into illness.

The Color of Rose

In the early evening, I painted clay,
Washing my brushes in a
Small, plastic tub.
Finishing and cleaning, there appeared,
In the residue of the paints used,
Small crystals of gold
And silver, and some of
Ice and rose.
My heart stirred at seeing these, for I was
Taken there, almost there, again,
From deep want of my senses:
The laughter of my little brownskins,
The silent sounds rippling
Over gold and silver
And ice and rose.
I kept my tears dry, and silenced any
Sound to my ears, inside and out;
I was happy in part, and in another
Part I was sad, and most,
I think,
I felt full in my heart,
So that it would burst. I could not remain composed.
From my pen, then, lifted young, innocent,
Joyfully unabridged laughter,
Gold, and silver, ice and rose.
Tomorrow,
The sun will rise, the first eye
To fall upon the glory of all creation,
Indeed, so from its own glory, and

Clouds, silver-white will appear
Above, icy dew below to sparkle,
And rose—rose
Is the color my mother gave to me.

Elizabeth

January 23, 2005

228

Concluding Sentiment

A year is a long time, a year is a short time; between its lengthiness and within its brevity lie many sayings about much feeling; and yesterday is constructed around its many movements. As the years continue their perpetual journey, our lives add frames with scenes of our mortal experience, with the immortal always close beside in thought and knowing. Our days become too filled, as does our thought, to readily access any one image with the wish, and recording becomes necessary to holding: the experiences, the sentiment, and attending reflection.

"Musings . . ." is just this record, in verse form, of the sentiments I experienced throughout the year, 2008, those which were, or did, in some fashion, insist on not being laid aside with the day. Very likely these insistencies were the callings of my secret places, those that had been visited in a course of hours and would not allow the deeper chambers of my heart to close their doors to them on finishing. It may have been a fragrance or melody, near or far, but as the mourning dove's poignant lament, held my whole self, in recognition and knowing. Just as likely, it could have been an exchange with fellows which was left a billowing up of thought and sentiment, as with an intimate embracing of the grande natural, buttressing my soul with wisdom and truth. It was not a special year, but special that it was.

My pen, I have remarked often to friends, is my best voice, for it sings eagerly, easily for me. Its verses may have merit only in furnishing my record to myself, but I would like to think that my cosem is friendly to all others, and that we can sing and reflect

229

together happily or with somber threads that wind throughout—for they are there with us all—but that we sing: hearts enjoined, moments, however brief or extended, the reading, immortality issuing out the experience.

Elizabeth
February 14, 2009
About seven o'clock am
Valentine's Day

Printed in the United States
by Baker & Taylor Publisher Services